THE REAL THING

BALLANTINE BOOKS

NEW YORK

THE REAL THING

Lessons on Love and Life from a
Wedding Reporter's Notebook

Ellen McCarthy

The Real Thing is a work of nonfiction. Some names and identifying details have been changed.

Published in the United States by Ballantine Books, an imprint of Random House, a division of Random House LLC, a Penguin Random House Company, New York.

BALLANTINE and the HOUSE colophon are registered trademarks of Random House LLC.

LIBRARY OF CONGRESS CATALOGING-IN-PUBLICATION DATA
McCarthy, Ellen.
The real thing : lessons on love and life from a wedding reporter's notebook / Ellen McCarthy.
pages cm
ISBN 978-0-345-54969-3 (hardback)
ISBN 978-0-345-54970-9 (ebook)
1. Man-woman relationships. 2. Couples. 3. Interpersonal attraction. 4. Interpersonal relations. 5. Marriage. 6. McCarthy, Ellen
I. Title.
HQ801.M4854 2015
306.7—dc23   2014039901

Printed in the United States of America on acid-free paper

www.ballantinebooks.com

2 4 6 8 9 7 5 3 1

FIRST EDITION

Book design by Dana Leigh Blanchette
Title-page image: © iStockphoto.com

To Pat and Jude, who filled my world
with love from the start.

And to Aaron, who proved it was better than
I ever believed it could be.

Contents

COMMITMENT

BREAKUPS

WEDDINGS

MAKING IT LAST

Introduction

Every time I came to an intersection in the early summer of 2009 I stood still, patiently waiting for a bus to hit a pothole and shower me with mud. Never mind that it hadn't rained in weeks. The drenching was inevitable.

Having seen *Bridget Jones's Diary* and my share of *Sex and the City* episodes, I knew what was coming. I just had to hope it would end in a late-night makeout session with some handsome Mr. Darcy.

My life, you see, had recently been hijacked by a chick-lit novel. And a poorly conceived one at that. In a single day I was hired to be the full-time weddings reporter for *The Washington Post* and broke up with my boyfriend of eighteen months. Obviously I was thirty at the time.

In the weeks that followed I could feel myself slipping further and further into the realm of total cliché. Calling wedding planners and florists between crying jags in the ladies' room. Smiling through interviews with one happy couple after another while despairing that I would never experience that kind of joy. (My fear was confirmed in a bar a few weeks later when a gypsy woman asked if I'd like a palm reading. She took my ten dollars, grabbed my hand, and then looked at me with a strange mix of horror and pity. "I don't see a love line," she told me. *"It's not there."*)

I'll spare you the suspense. I did not move home to live with my parents or convene an emergency roundtable of cosmo-sipping friends. I never even got soaked by a bus. I did become the walking target for an unusual number of bird droppings that summer, but that wasn't so bad. At least it was my own sad-sack montage, not Katherine Heigl's.

And for the next four years I spent most of my Saturday nights at other people's weddings. I interviewed more than two hundred couples who were about to walk down the aisle and dozens of others who'd been together for decades. I got the chance to pick the brains of matchmakers, sex therapists, psychologists, neurologists, and philosophers who all spend their days investigating what makes relationships work.

And again and again, the lessons I learned on the job intersected with the events of my personal life.

During my time covering weddings I grieved and healed and went on first dates with half the men in Washington, D.C. Eventually I met the best one—for me, at least. And together, as I'll relate in this book, Aaron and I proceeded through the well-worn stages of modern romance: infatuation, living in sin, eight circles of wedding-planning hell, and, finally, the actual ever-after of wedded reality.

I'd been at the *Post* for nine years when the editors decided to create a new section dedicated to weddings. At the time, I was happily writing about arts and entertainment and was hesitant to apply for the position. It's an odd role at an ambition-fueled place like the *Post:* Weddings coverage isn't an obvious stepping-stone to the White House beat. But eventually I admitted to myself that I didn't really *want* the White House beat. I wanted to write about people.

This was a way to do it. And I'd be covering one of the most meaningful, intimate narratives anyone can have—how he or she found and recognized the person with whom they wanted to spend the rest of their life.

From the beginning I took the endeavor seriously. I understood that my pieces were candy for readers and that my job made me the newsroom cream puff. But couples were sharing extraordinarily personal details with me and trusting me to convey their tales with warmth and sensitivity. And I knew that these stories, unlike others I'd written, wouldn't just be used to wrap fish the day after they ran. These articles would be laminated and framed, passed down to grandchildren, and absorbed into family histories.

I also knew that some of them would provide hope. I'd always loved hearing how-we-met stories because they made me think, "Well, if it happened for this couple in that way, it could happen for me, too." There's some solace in knowing life isn't all mud puddles and bird shit, no?

The job was also intriguing because I'd always been somewhat obsessed with relationships. Maybe we all are. No matter how great things are going in other aspects of life—career, school, money, friends—if your relationship is in turmoil, everything else can feel irrelevant. And when you're blessed with the comfort of a strong partnership, life's worst travails can seem a little less brutal.

As much as I was fascinated by love, though, I was also baffled by it. With most things, hard work and determination usually lead to certain results. Study more and you'll get better grades. Train for a marathon and you'll eventually be able to complete one.

It's not always so simple with relationships. You can be "out there" for years without meeting your match. And as I'd just been reminded firsthand, you can make every effort imaginable to have a romance work out, but that doesn't guarantee it will. (Which, as we usually realize in retrospect, is almost always for the best.) The breakup I'd just gone through was as mutual, mature, and kind as any split can be, but it was still horrible. They all are.

In my life I'd already spent countless hours gnawing on the big questions with friends: "How will you know when you've found 'The One'?" "What if you never do?" "What's the secret to staying happy together over a lifetime?" What I didn't know when I began to report on weddings was that I'd meet my guides and gurus along the way. Each couple and expert I encountered seemed to offer some unique clue about the way love works. Kerilyn and Peter showed me that the road isn't always straight; Runy and Junie taught me the importance of taking risks; researcher Terri Orbuch revealed her ten-minute rule to maintaining emotional intimacy.

The people I met informed my approach to dating and helped me recognize the real thing when it finally came along. And by telling their stories they offered lessons on relationships and commitment that have become guiding principles in my own marriage.

Like any complicated subject—string theory, the enduring fame of the Kardashians—it often seems like the more you learn about love, the less you know for sure. But as my reporting continued over the years, I became increasingly convinced of one thing: We ask a lot more from relationships than we're willing to put into them.

Think of all the time we spend over the course of our lives studying nutritional information, celebrity breakdowns, and what not to wear. We want to know everything about everything. Except love—that, we continue to treat like magic fairy dust that should appear mysteriously, anoint us in rapture, and relieve all our late-night, Ben & Jerry's binge-eating sorrow. On top of that, we ask that it stick around forever—burning with passion and serving as the foundational rock of our lives and those of our children and our children's children.

That kind of thinking has helped no one but Maury Povich and the Divorce Lawyers of America. To that end, I'd like to suggest that this crazy little thing called love could benefit from a bit more investigation. So let's loosen our ties, unglue the fake lashes, and turn to the stories of others who can help us figure out what's going on here.

My husband always laughs when people refer to me as a relationship expert. He, better than anyone, knows that I'm not; it's all the-blind-leading-the-blind in this arena. But I've had the unique opportunity to follow around an awful lot of blind people, each one holding some little flicker of light. Taken together those sparks might just be enough to lead the way for the rest of us.

I'm profoundly grateful to the experts, couples, and other willing subjects I met during my time on the romance beat. They generously shared their most treasured stories and made an extraordinary, lasting impact on my life, offering wisdom I never could have accrued on my own. This book is a collection of those insights—on dating, commitment, breakups, weddings, and marriage—gifts that were given to me and that I hope will be of some service to you.

Because here is perhaps the most important thing I learned: Love is not (entirely) unknowable. We'll never unravel all its mysteries, of course, nor would we want to. But we can get better at and smarter about it, and increase our chances of creating happy, fulfilling relationships. We just have to be willing to listen to those who've gone before us.

Some of the insights in this book might be things you already know intuitively. But occasionally it helps to have someone else articulate a particular truth for it to really sink in. At least, it did for me.

And some lessons here may resonate less than others. That's the thing about truths—they're only true if they're true for you. So please, take whatever feels right, and good, to you. Use the rest as fireplace kindling—I'll be happy just knowing it kept you warm.

Because this relationship stuff is hard. Wonderful, curious, confounding, and *hard*. So wherever you are—single, dating, or already committed—my wish is that something you read here will somehow make it a little easier.

I hope most of all that you find whatever it is you're looking for. And that it makes your life infinitely richer, sweeter, and more rewarding.

May a bus never drench you with mud and a bird never poop on your head. Amen.

DATING

I didn't date much in my early twenties. I could say I was focused on my career and that's true, but it's also not relevant. My romantic life was nonexistent because I was scared of dating—at least as it seemed to work in the adult world.

In college I'd had exactly two boyfriends, both of whom I met the old-fashioned way . . . at keg parties, under the glow of neon beer signs and the influence of that greatest of all aphrodisiacs, grain alcohol. By evening's end there was a bit of fuzzy making out and then, somehow, we were together. (One of these blossoming relationships was tragically compromised when the gentleman in question sent my Christmas present, a silky little Victoria's Secret number, to my parents' house. I transferred to a different college the next semester, much to my father's delight.)

Dating in the real world seemed like a different ball game. One with a lot more rules, consequences, and potential for injury. I didn't want to hurt anyone, or be hurt, or face the awkward question of whether or not there should be a good-night kiss. So I didn't. I went to happy hours, occupied myself with a few private crushes, and felt just fine about staying in on a Saturday night.

But four or five years after graduation, I got lonely enough and finally waded into the murky waters of modern dating. I threw up an online profile, and met guys at bars and parties and through friends. By the time I was hired on the weddings beat I'd had a couple of relationships lasting a year or more and was pretty practiced at dating. Not that it stopped being awkward or fraught; I just built up a tolerance for those things.

I realized that going on dates was not so different from interviewing people for work. I once complained to my mother about how much I was dreading having dinner with a man I'd met online. "Oh, come on!" she said. "You get to get dressed up, go out, meet someone new!" Of course she said this from the comfort of her couch, from which she'd have to be dragged kicking and screaming to go make conversation with a stranger.

For some people dating really is fun. For the rest of us it's a means to an end—whether that end is sex, companionship, or matrimony. You run the gauntlet of rejection and dejection in the hope of finding whatever finish line you're after.

When I first started on the weddings beat—also starting, as I've mentioned, a new chapter of single life—I wasn't sure how it would affect me to spend my days interviewing deliriously happy couples and watching them walk down the aisle. It could have been like salt in a wound.

But the job had the opposite effect. All of these people—young, old, rich, poor, plain, beautiful, sophisticated, and simple—they'd all found someone. I was reminded again and again that love happens every day, *in all kinds of ways, to all kinds of people. And when it does, it adds a beauty and richness to life that nothing else can match.*

So a couple of months after the breakup, I found my dating legs again. This time I had the lessons of the people I'd written about swirling around in my head. Their experiences pushed me to be more open and optimistic, and to at least try to enjoy it.

Even more important, the collective wisdom of these couples challenged me to rethink what I was looking for. So much of what they taught me about love ran contrary to what we learn in pop culture and society. Don't look for lightning. Forget about presenting your best self—it's your real self that counts. And dreams do come true, but almost never how you dreamed them.

Screw Meeting Cute

This is how I came into being: In the mid-1970s my mom, a recent college graduate, took a teaching job at a small business institute in rural western New York. Suddenly this city girl was living in the kind of place where three cars in a turning lane constitutes a traffic jam, exciting Friday nights almost certainly involve high school football, and the stealthy scent of manure can strike at any time.

Her bosses at the school, an older married couple with eight kids, repeatedly asked to fix her up with one of their sons. She was flattered, I'm sure, but wanted absolutely no part of it.

Desperate to get out one weekend, she drove five hours across the state for a reunion with college friends in Albany. At their favorite neighborhood bar she held court, regaling them with tales of the backward hick town where she was living and the couple she worked for. Before long a blue-eyed guy from

the next table wandered over, prodding her to keep the outra-
geous stories coming. He let her go on for almost an hour before flatly informing her that he was her bosses' son.

"And," he said, "you're fired."

Oops?

He didn't fire her, of course. He bought her a Miller Lite
and then married her. They had my sister, my brother, and me
and have been drinking cheap beer together for forty-plus
years now.

Really sweet, right? Well, you try living under the tyranny
of that kind of love story your whole life. What could possibly
stack up against that? Perhaps I could marry a man who first
plowed me down with a bike and then used mouth-to-mouth
resuscitation to bring me back from the brink of death. Or a
guy who moved into my old apartment and tracked me down
across the world to return a precious locket I'd forgotten. I
needed to not just meet the right guy, but to meet him in the
right *way*. A Nora Ephron–worthy encounter that would be
indisputably full of charm, humor, and serendipity.

It took me about thirty years—and six months on the job as a
professional relationships reporter—to realize that how people meet doesn't have much bearing on how happy they are
together.

Of course, I was always looking for great how-we-met stories to write for the column. I'll never forget hearing a wounded Iraq veteran talk about falling in love with the pretty hospital volunteer who gave him the courage to learn to walk on his new prosthetic legs. I swooned over the couple who met on a train—it was her birthday and she was on the phone complaining about another guy who'd been sending mixed signals—when he slipped her a note asking, "Will you go out with me? Circle one. Yes. No. Maybe." And I instantly loved the two women who fell for each other after sparring as contestants on *Jeopardy!* (Their wedding program aptly thanked Alex Trebek for his matchmaking skills.)

But eventually I became just as interested in the pairs who'd been close friends for years before their feelings shifted. And the classmates who never noticed each other until they were assigned to the same project. The couples who met a million times before it clicked. Because in each instance *something happened*. Something that changed their lives indelibly. And there is as much mystery and wonder in the quieter stories as those with some dramatic twist of fate.

Moreover—and I realize this is probably much more obvious to you than it was to me—the way we meet is almost entirely irrelevant. Of course the stories we tell about ourselves matter, mostly in the way they shape our thinking about our own lives. A couple who feels that the whole universe conspired to bring them together might be more likely to fight for their union than a pair who hooked up at 3 A.M. in a bar because there didn't seem to be anyone better around. But even the grandest sense of fate will not do the dishes or stop a roving eye or hold your hair back when you're sick with the flu.

For a Valentine's Day edition one year, the *Post* put out a call for six-word love stories. There was one that always stuck with me: "Arranged marriage. Two kids. Happy family."

You meet once. For an instant, an hour or an evening. It's the ever-after that goes on, hopefully, for a lifetime. And those years are made up of many moments—magical and mundane—that mean so much more than the first.

Incidentally, I met Aaron at a party in the middle of a blizzard. We cracked jokes for most of the night and shared a cab home. He tried to kiss me but didn't ask for my number. The next morning I woke up hungover but smiling, and racked my wine-soaked brain to figure out why. Once I remembered, I sent him a friend request on Facebook. And the rest is—well, you know.

After we'd been dating for about a year, a woman at a holiday party asked to hear the story of our first meeting. Once we had relayed our tale her face fell and she dryly suggested we either improve the delivery or come up with a lie. We're working on both.

But in truth, I don't really care if she didn't like our story. It's ours. I still feel a rush of warmth whenever I think about that night. And it doesn't even begin to compare with what I feel about all the nights that followed.

"The One"

I felt like I'd tripped into the world of *Gulliver's Travels* when I met Betty and Edgar. They opened the door together and stared up at me as if I were the world's tallest woman. Between my three-inch heels and five-feet-eight-inch frame, I hovered about a foot above the tops of their gray heads.

"Well, come on back," Edgar said as he and Betty turned with their canes to lead me to a living room filled with books, board games, and stacks of *The New Yorker* that looked as if they'd actually been read, not just accumulated.

By the time I met them, Betty was eighty-four and Edgar was eighty-six. They'd been married for sixty-five years. I'd come there to learn the secret of their success, but it seemed that they were as impressed as anyone that the relationship had worked out.

In 1942, Edgar, a Pittsburgh native, had jumped in his car and driven a couple of hours north to Erie after a friend told him he should "date Betty Shapiro—she's fun!" Betty *was* fun. She was also sharp and witty and had quick comebacks for all of his best lines. They went out twice before Edgar shipped off with the army.

They mostly fell out of touch after that, but when Betty heard from a friend that Edgar was sick with pneumonia in Sioux Falls, South Dakota, and that the doctors didn't think he would make it, she wrote him a three-word letter: "Carry on, kid."

Edgar survived the illness and soon the two were writing back and forth regularly. Betty visited Edgar in Wisconsin and then in Florida, where he asked her to get married. She couldn't see any reason why not. So the couple caught an afternoon matinee, exchanged vows in a rabbi's office, and celebrated over dinner in a "dinky restaurant" with Betty's two cousins and "the bimbos" they'd brought as dates. She was nineteen then. He was one year older and about to ship off to war.

"And that was the glorious wedding!" Betty exclaimed, pointing a finger in the air six and a half decades later.

"I wouldn't give you twenty cents for the chances of that marriage lasting," Edgar told me.

But of course it did, though in some ways the two were very different from each other. Betty was organized and serious. She worked as a business manager and had, according to Edgar, "the mind of a CEO and a CFO." A researcher at the Library of Congress, Edgar was creative and artistic, often acting in plays, writing poems, and dreaming up new projects around the house (some of which he even completed).

I sat for several hours with the pair, who had the kind of teasing, rat-a-tat-tat rapport that only comes from decades of togetherness. They were sharp, funny, and—most important for me as a journalist—deeply candid.

They told me how hard it was at the start of their marriage and how it took them twenty-three years to save enough money to buy a house. They talked about the joy of raising their son, Howard, and the way they got through fights— Betty smoked her cigarettes, Edgar occasionally went to the garage to let out a scream of frustration. "But even if you're angry, you still kiss each other," Betty said.

They couldn't get over the way time seemed to evaporate. Now there were cataracts and bifocals and life was increasingly marked by doctors' appointments, but they didn't feel old. They still sat close on the couch and patted each other on the knee in appreciation of a good joke. "If you can't laugh easily and cry easily, all is lost," Betty said with a shrug.

Before I got up to leave, I mentioned that people in my generation talk a lot about "The One"—the idea that everyone has a single person out there in the world meant just for them. Surely Betty and Edgar had found that in each other.

Ha! They stared at me like I'd sprouted a second head and then they laughed and laughed and laughed. Hogwash!

"Had we married other people," Edgar said, "I believe, being who we are, we would've been married for sixty-five years to those other people." It wasn't fate or serendipity that created their lasting marriage; it was commitment.

Once Edgar even met an ex-boyfriend of Betty's. Betty and Edgar had both been nervous the encounter would be awkward. But the two men adored each other and talked for hours—Betty couldn't get a word in edgewise. "We had a ball," Edgar remembered.

"You tend toward loving the same kind of person," Betty said. "But there are some people who are never satisfied with anything."

If you're waiting for the perfect person, they agreed, you'd better get used to waiting. "What are you youngsters thinking?" Betty asked, shaking her head as she walked me toward the door. "There's no Greek god that's going to come down and save you."

And who needs a Greek god, anyway, if you can have a mortal love like theirs?

Good on Paper
(But Not Good Enough for You)

Sarah nearly didn't go out with Alex. Hell, she might not have even responded to his message if she hadn't been at her parents' house, with her mother looking over her shoulder, prodding, "But he's so cute!"

Sarah had very clearly specified in her profile that she was looking for a guy over six feet tall with brown hair and brown eyes. Alex had blond hair, blue eyes, and was just five feet eight. "Obviously he didn't read my criteria," Sarah remembered thinking. (For the record, she's five two.)

To appease her mother, she replied to Alex's message, peppering him with questions: "If you could go on vacation to one place, where would you go?" "What are the three things you'd bring with you on a desert island?" "What color would your voice be if it were a color?"

Alex got her attention when he gamely answered "plaid." They emailed intermittently and eventually set up a coffee date, but Sarah, a school psychologist, was sure it wouldn't go anywhere. She'd recently begun seeing another man she was excited about. And he was perfect—on paper. He was everything she'd always said she wanted in a guy. She'd known him forever and the two had always promised they'd get together if they were single at the same time. Plus, he was taller than five eight. It felt fated.

Just as she expected, her first date with Alex was a bust. They got mixed up about which bookstore they were supposed to meet in and both were too tired from recent travels to pull off any sparkling conversation. But when he asked for a do-over, she agreed to give it one more chance and have dinner together. That time something clicked. They talked without pause for six hours and quickly made plans to see each other again.

Alex was a government analyst with a mischievous grin and a twinkle in his eye. He brought out Sarah's silly side and made her laugh. When a bar was too crowded, they went to a nearby pharmacy and read each other quizzes from *Cosmopolitan* magazine. Being with him felt familiar and exciting at the same time. Within a month the other guy was out of the picture.

Because here is the thing about "good on paper"—it is completely irrelevant.

I once interviewed a woman in her fifties who, after thirty years of marriage, laughed about how inane her list of desired qualities turned out to be. She wanted a guy who looked a certain way and came from a certain background. "Humor, kindness, generosity of spirit—none of that was on my list," she told me. "And yet those were the ingredients that made for a healthy relationship that endured a lot of tough times."

Good on paper is all about externals: a person's pedigree, occupation, income, status, appearance. But those things won't keep you warm at night, rub your back when you're exhausted, or know just what to say when you're sad. They won't bring out the hidden layers of yourself that you usually keep from the rest of the world.

In truth, the things that make someone good on paper might not even have much to do with you. Not the real you. They probably have more to do with what other people expect for you, the kind of image you want to project at cocktail parties or the credentials that will sound good in a *New York Times* wedding announcement. That's why blind dates so rarely work out—they're the result of somebody else's estimation of who you should be with, not your own inscrutable but deeply knowing internal compass.

So forget good on paper. Or, at the very least, be skeptical when you find yourself in a relationship with a walking, talking résumé.

It Won't Come in the Package
You're Expecting

Leigh always dated Jewish guys—and assumed, of course, that she would marry one.

So you can imagine her surprise when she fell in love during business school with a tall Florida native of Indian origin. Leigh, who has a lilting voice and the face of a porcelain doll, was initially put off by Devu's gregariousness. But his humor grew on her as they spent time together and she found herself more relaxed with him than she'd ever felt with anyone.

He made her loosen up, let go of her rigid ways, and forgo study sessions and gym time for spontaneous adventures around Chicago. Then, after a few months of dating, he broke up with her. He had to, he told her, because he needed to be with someone Indian.

So you can imagine *my* surprise when, on the day before their wedding, as Leigh told me this story while the freshly painted mehndi dried on her hands, Devu's mother walked into their hotel suite. She had the loving energy of a sixties flower child. She was also white.

I looked at Leigh to register my confusion. "I know," she said, with arched eyebrows.

Dating an Indian woman wasn't a family requirement, but Devu's own. After breaking up with Leigh, he did go on to date an Indian woman, who turned out to be a terrible fit for him. It wasn't until Leigh and Devu started hanging out again—on a school trip to India, ironically—that he realized he was meant to be with Leigh and that her ancestry didn't matter.

"But what about you?" I asked her. "Was it hard to move past the fact that Devu isn't Jewish?"

"Not really," Leigh said with a shrug. She explained that a married friend had once told her that the right guy would never come in the package she expected. "I always remembered that," she said.

My father recently reminded me that throughout my twenties, my long list of husband-to-be requirements included the following: older, Irish, Catholic, fan of the Buffalo Bills. That's right—anyone hoping to apply for the position had to actively root for the Bills. Never mind how painful an endeavor that usually is, or that I myself couldn't name a single player on the team and hadn't watched an entire game in years. I knew exactly who my future husband would be. Now I just had to find

the man I'd created in my mind. The Bills specification nar-
rowed the pool, but I still found plenty of men who *looked* like
the right guy from a distance.

Of course, it never worked out. I wasn't smart enough, like
Leigh or her friend, to ditch my preconceived notions. At least
not then.

For several years I was involved in a long-standing D.C. singles
tradition called FriendSwap—first as a dater, then as an orga-
nizer. The idea is that every year a group of singles invite all
their other single pals to a party, so everyone in attendance is
vetted. And in advance of the party, each person fills out a
basic questionnaire about who they are and what they're looking for in a mate. Then organizers match up each single with
four or five potential dates who seem like a good fit.

The system works remarkably well, resulting in an average
of one marriage a year. But here's the thing: People are insane. This became abundantly clear during the years I volunteered as a matchmaker. Really, five-foot-two lady? You
absolutely *refuse* to date men under six one? And you, forty-
eight-year-old divorced father of three? You can't conceive of
going out with a woman over thirty-five? Yes, we're very proud
of you Ms. J.D./Ph.D./M.D., but does your future husband
really have to possess an equivalent degree? Not surprisingly,
these are the folks who came back to the party year after year

because they just couldn't seem to find what they were looking for.

It's not that I don't think there's merit to daydreaming or knowing what you want. It's that couples like Leigh and Devu convinced me there's a real danger in becoming a prisoner to those ideas. It automatically restricts your pool. And more important, there's a good chance that what you want is not what you actually need.

Aaron was in his late twenties when we met. I was two and a half years older. He wasn't lunatic enough to set his requirements in stone the way I had, but he was a handsome Jewish guy whose vague notions of an ideal future wife didn't include words like "older" and "Catholic." So even after a great first date, I continued to go out with other guys who looked, *on paper,* like much better matches. But each date fell flat. Conversation never flowed the way it did with him. None of the other men left me laughing quite as hard or wanting to extend the evening for just one more beer.

The more we hung out, over weeks and then months, the more we realized that everything that really mattered was there, just beneath the packaging.

And for the record, Aaron has come around and now considers himself a Bills fan. He likes them in the same way one likes a wounded bird trying to stay aloft, but that's fine. We'll take what we can get.

Never Say Never

Quit using words like *never, only,* and *must.* As in: "I would never date someone who owns cats." "I only date carnivores—sanctimonious vegetarians need not apply." "Whoever I marry must love world travel as much as I do."

On second thought, stick to your guns. It's funnier that way.

Just ask Nikki, a hardworking African American technology manager I interviewed a few years ago. She was single and in her early thirties when she told friends that she had just one requirement for her future husband: that he be "someone who will reach the high things on the shelf."

Then she fell in love with a little person. Standing side by side, Daniel comes up not quite to her shoulders. That he is also a Jewish white boy is further proof that our benevolent God occasionally likes to say, "Ha!"

The two first met at a casual happy hour and stayed in touch sporadically via email for a few years. As Nikki's friends were starting to get married and have children, she decided she needed to broaden her social circle and shot Dan a note asking if he wanted to get together.

The first concert they attended was awkward and Nikki went home disappointed—it seemed like he wouldn't even be friend material. But when they got together again with a larger group they found themselves gravitating toward each other and laughing at the same moments. After a couple of months of incessant emailing and ambiguous outings, they finally kissed.

Nikki, who'd already done well enough to buy a home on her own, is sharp, funny, and doesn't suffer fools. And throughout her twenties she'd developed a habit of finding *something* wrong with each guy she dated. Anybody else might not even notice the flaw, but for Nikki it was always a disqualifier.

"I have a low tolerance for lots of things," she told me. "But Dan just never drove me crazy."

Dan is quiet but deeply caring, and he broke open a tenderness in Nikki. Once she really let him in, they quickly fell for each other.

The pair weathered a health crisis when Dan developed a seizure disorder that required multiple surgeries and many teary nights in the hospital. They were nearly driven apart over differences of opinion on whether to have children—she wanted them, he wasn't so sure. But ultimately they overcame that, too, as Dan spent time with small children and came around to the idea.

Today Dan and Nikki are married with a beautiful little boy and a life rich with laughter. They have been together for nearly a decade now, and Dan has never been the one to reach the high things on the shelf for Nikki.

"That's how I know I really love him," she told me. "Because I don't care."

It happens all the time. People wind up with someone who pushes them outside their box of preconceived notions. And they're happier for it.

I loved talking to the atheist who refused to go out with anyone religious—until she met a handsome Catholic man who liked her as much as he liked God. A British man couldn't imagine dating a South Asian woman—a prejudice he attributed to "colonial stuff" that had been "bred into me at boarding school"—and naturally wound up with a sweet Nepali woman. I've covered the weddings of countless liberal-loathing Republicans and Bush-hating Democrats who fell in love across party lines. And I live in Washington, D.C., where people take politics—and themselves—very seriously.

One of my favorite interviews was with one of Elvis Presley's former girlfriends (really!), who swore not only never to marry, but also to never get involved with any student at her ballroom dance studio. Then she fell in love with a former Green Beret who kept enrolling in her classes—and staying late for more time with his teacher. She was sixty-four on the day of their peacock-themed wedding. He was thirty-one.

So go ahead, keep on telling the universe exactly what you will and won't do. You might end up old and alone. More likely, though, you'll wind up married to an agoraphobic, cat-loving vegan who's never owned a passport. But you won't mind. You'll be in love.

Do: Go Online Already

I met Julie and Andrew a couple of months after getting hired on the weddings beat. We sat down together in a specialty chocolate shop that featured overpriced truffles and soft jazz music.

Andrew and Julie were, like the confections, almost achingly sweet. Their story was marked with the kind of quirky serendipity usually found in Zooey Deschanel movies.

Julie was a classic beauty with an air of refinement. Her first marriage, to an old high school flame, had ended in a wrenching divorce. After grieving for months, she moved from Boston to D.C., hoping for a fresh start. For the first time in her adult life, the thirty-two-year-old was learning to date.

That meant putting in time with a string of duds, including one who stood her up and another who spent the whole night trying to shove his tongue down her throat. Then came Andrew, a longtime bachelor with a shaved head, a goatee, and a dog named Beauford. Julie was a lawyer; Andrew was a law librarian. They both loved Gothic architecture, spicy food, and classical music. And, almost instantly, they loved each other.

"He's the greatest gift I've ever been given," she told me, gazing at Andrew across the table the week of their wedding. "Beyond dreams, beyond imagination."

To this day, I have never met a couple more desperately, fully in love. Or more sure that they were meant to be—drawn together by inexplicable cosmic forces. And what timeless vehicle did the universe choose to unite these young lovers? The Internet; eHarmony, to be specific. I suspect 35 to 40 percent of the couples applying to be written about in my wedding column met online—and the numbers are only increasing. And all of the couples who got together with a little help from technology feel the same sense of fate as couples who met while serving on a Peace Corps mission or while sharing a wall as next-door neighbors.

eHarmony matched Julie and Andrew on a Wednesday. By ten that morning they'd completed all of the site's required steps of communication and begun a rapid-fire volley of emails. They traded puns and talked about his childhood as the son of diplomats. On a date that Friday, he watched her add hot sauce to her salsa at a Mexican restaurant and thought, "Oh God, I think I might be in love."

Moral of the story: If you're looking for love—or an occasional good time or a series of horrifying anecdotes to amuse friends with during happy hour—please just go online already.

I realize online dating is the adult version of an eighth-grade dance and that it's a major time-suck and a black hole of rejection and ambiguity and lies. But it also works. Not every time, but often enough—as I've seen firsthand through my reporting—that it's worth getting over your hang-ups and trying it. Especially since we don't live in an era where your aunt Marge is going to introduce you to every available bachelor or bachelorette in a thirty-mile radius.

The Internet hasn't created any foolproof ways to guarantee love for life, but it does at least offer opportunities to meet new people. To a large extent dating is a numbers game—you've got to kiss a lot of frogs. And God knows there's nowhere you can find more frogs than the Internet.

I probably tried a half dozen dating sites—including eHarmony, of course, after meeting Andrew and Julie. And you could say it didn't work for me. Mostly I just went on bad dates. (See chapter titled "Online Dates to Avoid.")

For each outing I put on lipstick and got my hopes up, only to feel sinking disappointment as I took a swig of wine and concluded that this guy, too, was not the one. It's exhausting. (The occasional hiatus from online dating seems crucial to prevent burnout, or a complete psychotic break.) But what it did for me, even if it didn't deliver a long-term love, was keep me optimistic that I would find one. It was a constant reminder of how many guys there are in the world and that I didn't know all of them. That the right one could be around the next corner or on the next page of profiles. And that I should keep looking.

Julie and Andrew lived in my neighborhood, so I ran into them occasionally after their gorgeous wedding at the National Cathedral. I loved seeing Julie's belly grow round and then Andrew pushing a baby carriage. Today they have two girls, a house they've named the Eyrie, and enduring gratitude for the life that online dating has given them.

It might only give you a string of horror stories about the basest specimens of humanity, but you never know. It could lead to so much more.

Don't: Treat Match.com
Like Amazon

If I could impart just one message to online daters the world over, it would be this: People. Aren't. Shoes.

A study led by Eli J. Finkel, a social psychologist at Northwestern University, found that online dating causes people to adopt more of a shopping mentality when it comes to finding a mate. Singles who use dating websites become more judgmental. They also reduce potential dates to a collection of quantifiable characteristics—height, age, income level, etc.—rather than whole, complicated, multilayered human beings.

I remember when I heard that a friend of a friend discovered her longtime boyfriend had recently put up an online dating profile. It was headlined, "Bored in My Current Relationship." We were all horrified, though I thought he'd done every woman online a great service by declaring his moral bankruptcy right up front.

I think the greatest danger of online dating—beyond the possibility of being abducted by a charismatic serial killer—is this potential to turn the search for meaningful human connection into an exercise in superficial window-shopping. Obviously, dating websites have done extraordinary good by bringing together large pools of eligible people. But they've also created the illusion that there is a never-ending supply of options guaranteed to offer a perfect fit.

As with a late-model television, that guy wasn't happy with his old relationship, so he figured he could just hop online to find a new one. And certainly, a ten-minute scan of profiles on a dating site could give anyone the impression that there are thousands of attractive singles waiting breathlessly to meet them.

Dr. Finkel says the window-shopping attitude may backfire in unexpected ways. That's because people think they know what they want in a mate, but they're not always right. A woman who limits her search to men over five feet eleven (remember Sarah and Nikki?) may miss out on a five-ten soul mate who could have made her happier than she'd ever dreamed.

Even the sheer number of options online dating presents is problematic. You're probably familiar with that oft-cited principle, the paradox of choice. People who were offered just a few flavors of ice cream were happier with their selection—and had an easier time committing to it—than those who had dozens of choices. It's not much different with dates—why stick with one person when there are so many other options right at your fingertips?

I think most people have the emotional intelligence to override the inclination to treat online dating sites like a commodities marketplace. But it's worth reminding ourselves every so often that there are real, breathing, thinking humans on the other end of those hazy bathroom mirror selfies. If you can't treat them the way you'd want to be treated, at least treat them the way you'd want your best friend's highly annoying but good-hearted younger brother to be treated—with an eye roll, compassion, and some small measure of kindness.

Online Dates to Avoid

I'd like to offer a few notes of hard-earned caution from years when I used every major dating site available, often simultaneously. In that span I went on more first dates than I care to remember and exactly one that eventually led to both a second and third date. Like every other veteran online dater, I generally stuck to coffee or drinks for the initial meeting. That way, after buckling under the wave of defeat we both felt upon meeting each other, the forced small talk could be contained to under an hour. Because, as Larry David once said: "A date is an experience you have with another person that makes you appreciate being alone."

Online daters will encounter plenty of tragicomic scenarios and abominations of humanity. But there's no use stepping on land mines I've already triggered, so I'd like to recommend you avoid the following red flags.

1. Anyone whose profile contains more than five instances of the word *fuck*. It may seem intriguingly Hunter S. Thompsonesque on the screen, but in person it translates to an angry every-other-word "motherfucker," sometimes actually used to describe the subject's own mother.

2. The person whose smile looks vaguely familiar. Your best friend dated him four years ago. He was creepy then and has grown creepier with age.

3. Anyone whose primary photo is even a tiny bit hazy. Since everyone now owns a phone that contains a professional-grade camera, this means he or she just *really* liked that shot from ten years ago. They will show up fatter, older, and wearing a teal button-down shirt. I promise.

4. People who list their exact salary. If you're looking for more slime in your life, take a mud bath instead.

5. The older foreigner who boasts about his seven-bedroom mansion and mentions needing a "lady of the house."

6. Anyone who looks even slightly rodentlike in photos. This never gets better in person.

7. Anyone who mentions an interest in "social dynamics." This actually means "I have had serious trouble with the opposite sex and thus spent many hours and a few

thousand dollars trying to learn to become a pickup artist." There will be misogyny and plenty of overly familiar touching before you have the chance to run.

8. The guy who writes about "really being ready to settle down now." He's still getting over his ex. (But you probably won't come across him anyway, because we talked it out for hours and he cried a lot, but by the end he decided to try to win her back. I hope, for all our sakes, she took him.)

Let's Get Chemical

Chemistry. It's the bane of every matchmaker's existence—crucially important, but impossible to predict, fake, or manufacture.

Even more frustrating is that no one knows fully what it is, or what causes it. But modern research has discovered that at least one important component of chemistry is, well . . . chemistry. And biology.

Researchers have found, for example, that women prefer different types of men depending on what point they happen to be at in their menstrual cycle. (When a woman is ovulating, a manly man is more likely to get a second look than the sensitive, brooding poet with refined cheekbones.) It works in the reverse, too. A pole dancer can expect to find a few extra dollars in her G-string when she's at the peak of her fertility cycle.

One of the most interesting studies I've seen, conducted by a Swiss biologist, required men to wear the same T-shirt to bed two nights in a row, sans deodorant. Women were then asked to smell the shirts and rate the attractiveness of their scents. The researchers found that the subjects preferred the smell of men whose genetic makeup was different from their own. Evolutionarily this makes sense: Children of parents with very different genetic backgrounds are more likely to be healthy, with stronger immune systems. (It also makes sense because incest is gross—scientifically speaking.)

Naturally, one enterprising capitalist immediately seized upon this information and launched—what else?—a dating company. You swab the inside of your cheek, potential partners swab theirs, and one quick genetic analysis later you're on your way to happily ever after and a sure bet of superhuman progeny.

All of this new information points to a singular conclusion: Emailing and texting for weeks before a first date is a fool's errand. The next time you meet a new love interest online, set up your meeting as soon as possible. Because science suggests your pheromones have veto power over your heart and head anyway. You might as well let them in on the process sooner, rather than later.

Get Out

When he was on the market, Aaron—who likes to claim I pulled him from his prime dating years—had one rule for himself. At least once each week he'd put himself in a position to meet someone new. It could be at a party or happy hour or cultural event—anything where there was guaranteed to be people he didn't know, hopefully of the single variety.

That way, he figured, he'd done his part. The rest was up to some higher power.

I always thought that was smart—and more ambitious than it appears at first glance. It's much easier to sit at home, or to stay wrapped in the warm cocoon of close friends and family. But those are also good ways to guarantee you won't find what—or who—you're looking for.

Don't Panic

In my first months on the weddings beat, as I healed from my recent breakup, I started waking up in the middle of the night with a fear that felt like a clamp squeezing my heart, sending waves of hot terror to my extremities. *"What if it never happens?"* I wondered. *"What if I never meet my husband?"*

The fear came so often and with such force that if I had redirected all the mental energy I spent worrying about my romantic future toward more pressing concerns, I probably could have cured cancer and created world peace—simultaneously.

But I couldn't get rid of the panic. And I don't know any noninvasive ways to help anyone else do it, either.

I did recognize that it was damaging, though, and not just because desperation is the aphrodisiac equivalent of raw sewage. It's a giant waste of time, yes. And much more insidiously, it has the potential to cloud our better judgment.

I suspect we can all think of couples who got together or chose to tie the knot because, at the time, it seemed like the only available choice. There was parental pressure, perhaps, or all their friends had coupled up. Maybe the alarm on their biological clock was blaring and it seemed like now or never, so—as they never exactly admitted out loud—*this will have to do.* "Letting things play out" and "gathering more information" never feel like viable options when one is operating in crisis mode.

I remember sitting with an acquaintance at lunch once. He was weeks away from getting married. To keep the conversation going I asked about the wedding and how he'd met his bride. The story that came back was something vaguely like: "Well, we have friends in common and she was nice and she wanted to get married and we're in our thirties so here we are." I had never met anyone so lukewarm about their betrothed, though this was before I started writing about weddings for a living. (Hint: If, when asked why you love someone, you draw a total blank, perhaps you should not marry them.)

My point is that fear isn't the best position from which to make major life decisions. So do whatever you can to beat it back. Maybe that means meditating, talking to a wise friend (or therapist), or trying to find humor in the fact that you've had seven bad dates in seven days (instead of deciding that it's the universe's way of saying that you should've married Grandma's neighbor's son when you had the chance).

For me, the thing that helped the most—and it's not for

everyone—was ten thousand dollars' worth of hormone injections and one minimally invasive outpatient procedure. I was thirty-one when I froze my eggs. I'd always known I wanted children and the night terrors were getting to be too much. It felt like a race against time and as my ninth-grade track coach can tell you, I've never been quick to the finish line.

My friends had mixed reactions to my decision, but to me it just made sense. This would stop the clock—at least for a little while. And it would prevent me from making a decision out of fear rather than love.

By the time I met Aaron I'd been saving up for the procedure for several months. I didn't mention it to him at first, worried that it would freak him out—I was already an older woman. Did I want him to know I also intended to put my future children on ice? But when I finally told him my plans, I was amazed by his reaction. He was supportive and even encouraging. Frankly, it took the pressure off both of us—the relationship could develop in its own time, not according to the strictures of those pesky fertility charts.

Again, I know this is not an option for everyone. It took me almost a year to put enough funds into a health savings plan to cover the procedure and even then I had to rely on my family for help when the medications were more expensive than I'd expected.

But it worked. Once my eggs were tucked safely into a freezer in suburbia, I felt a new sense of calm. It freed me. I knew that even if I never found the right partner—or simply didn't make it down the aisle for another decade—I still had the potential to create a family.

I've interviewed so many people who didn't find the right person until after they'd fully accepted the possibility that he or she might never come along. Once they were okay with that idea and could imagine a fulfilling life that included friends and family and work and pets and travel—but not necessarily a spouse—something broke open. And then someone came along.

But first they had to find a way to tamp down the panic. Often it happened out of exhaustion—they just *couldn't* worry about it anymore. And they realized the angst had never done them much good in the first place.

So, if you can, try to find a way to save yourself the trouble and the night terrors—you'll be better served by beauty sleep than worry lines.

The Truth: It Doesn't Happen
for Everyone

Now that I've suggested you try not to panic, I'm going to tell you something that will almost certainly cause you to panic. I'm sorry about that. But here is the truth: Not everyone finds the love of their life.

I wish it weren't this way. And I deeply hope it won't be this way for you or your children or your children's children. But it is the case for some people.

On a frigid New Year's Day my first year on the love beat, I was getting ready to go to the glamorous wedding of a former NBA player. He was marrying a chatty special education teacher he'd met a decade earlier. They'd been friends (with benefits) for years, but when she told him she was pregnant with his child, he didn't react the way she'd hoped. Eventually their relationship disintegrated into animosity. She resented him so much she refused to let anyone say his name in her presence. It went on that way for four years until they met to

discuss child support payments. As they talked something soft-
ened. He'd done a lot of growing up; she'd gathered the grace
to forgive. Scared of what people would think, they kept their
relationship secret until they couldn't bear it anymore. Then
they wanted to shout it from the rooftop. By the time the wedding rolled around, more than five hundred guests were expected at the ceremony.

See, nothing happens quite how you expect it! I'll never
forget that wedding because I was gripped with pulsating fear
the entire night. By then I'd been reporting for seven months
on couples getting married. I'd also been single for seven
months. As I drove to the wedding it struck me—I spent all my
time writing about people who find lasting love, but what
about the folks who don't get so lucky? No one talks about
them—about what their lives are like.

I'd never been so immediately, thoroughly terrified of a
story idea. That's how I knew I had to write it.

But I really didn't want to. I didn't want to intimately examine a fate I deeply feared for myself. And here is the shameful part: I didn't pursue the story until I'd met Aaron. It was
nearly two years after I had the initial idea and by then we'd
fallen in love and were on our way to marriage. I could tell you
I had other stories lined up that had to come first and that's
true. But it's also true that I wasn't brave enough while I was
still single to write a story about people who never find love.

———

Before I became the weddings reporter, I wrote about arts and entertainment and regularly interviewed celebrities with new movies coming out. (The dish: Sylvester Stallone is the sweetest, Kevin Costner is cocky, and someday I hope to be best friends with Queen Latifah, hanging out at her mansion and listening to vinyl records while discussing our favorite Maya Angelou poems.)

One day I met with the actor Jon Voight, who had come to Washington to promote a strange movie about a Mormon massacre that I'm pretty sure was never released. Our conversation somehow turned to relationships. (It's possible I've always been a *little* preoccupied with the subject.) Voight, who is twice divorced, became wistful and said he didn't think everyone gets to have a great love. That maybe it wouldn't happen for everyone in a particular lifetime, but they'd find it in a next life, and that for the time being they're meant to love their children or their pets or other people in need.

The thought knocked the wind out of me. Everyone spends all this time looking for their "other half" and some people just come up empty? That can't be right. But of course it is. I had great-aunts and neighbors who never married, and coworkers who were perpetually single, despite their efforts.

When I finally started reporting my story, I emailed one of my most loyal readers. Aviva is a successful documentary filmmaker and total romantic. She read my wedding stories every week and then called her girlfriends to discuss. She was raised on silver-screen love stories and had personally matched up ten married couples. Still dark-haired and vibrant at sixty-five, she desperately wanted a husband herself and though she'd had serious relationships in the past, none had lasted.

After interviewing Aviva, I flew to Los Angeles to meet with an elegant woman named Wendy who writes a blog about her single life. She was fifty-eight at the time, but daily ballet classes had kept her toned and agile. She was attractive, insightful, and warm. She wore chic boyfriend jeans, had just finished beautifully decorating her new condo at the foot of the Hollywood Hills, and, as we were talking on her couch, the deliveryman showed up with a pair of strappy couture heels that I found equally impressive and intimidating.

Wendy always assumed she'd marry. Her parents had a strong marriage. Her brother grew up to become a great husband. She had wonderful boyfriends in college and early adulthood. She dated all sorts of guys and kept a packed social calendar as she pursued a career in the arts. Wendy never doubted that family life was in her future until she went through a breakup at thirty-six that brought her the first twinges of worry.

Wendy still hoped she'd find the right guy, but in the meantime, she became an expert at navigating single life. Her calendar was always full. She organized holiday dinners at her place and always had the name of a great handyman in her Rolodex. She knew how to have fun at weddings even when she was the only person attending solo. Her blog was meant to be a space to share her thoughts and advice with others, and to destigmatize single life.

"There is so much sadness and guilt and shame," she told me, as her dog, Rosie, curled beside her on the couch. "I think if you could just take some of that away it would make the whole thing a lot easier."

As I spent time with Aviva, Wendy, and several other singles who never found the kind of love they were looking for, I realized that despite significant heartache, their lives were fulfilling and deeply satisfying. I also interviewed a few people who never wanted marriage and couldn't conceive of anything other than a single life, but they seemed to be in a different category. The people who interested me most did everything they could to find a mate—dated frequently, led active social lives, asked friends to set them up—and nothing had worked out.

But what both women wanted me to know was that they'd found ways to be happy, even though life hadn't unfolded exactly as they'd planned. They had huge social circles, deep relationships with family and friends, careers and hobbies they loved, and homes that were truly their own. Though they were both still open to love, they'd stopped waiting for it to complete them.

"I've survived and had a really full, rich, interesting life," Wendy said. "Part of writing about it is spreading the good news: Move on, there's nothing to pity here."

Their lesson was not to stay in limbo. When you're single, it can feel as if you won't know where your life is truly headed until you figure out who will be in it. What if you bite the bullet and buy your own home in one place only to meet a partner who wants to live somewhere else? What if you really want an advanced degree but worry that going back to graduate school will take up your free nights and impede your ability to date? Should you invest in the set of dishes you really want instead of hoping to one day get them as a wedding present?

Please, just do it. If you're waiting for someone else to come along before beginning your life, you risk never leaving the gate. Live where you want to live; do the things you want to do; surround yourself with people you love, who love you back. Of all the people I've interviewed, no one ever told me they felt that leading a full life held them back from finding love. Only the opposite. They were better able to love—themselves and others—when they fully embraced the life that was right in front of them.

If It Feels Like a Chess Match,
It's Probably Only a Game

I was moderating a panel discussion on dating and relationships when a woman in her twenties walked up to the microphone and asked for advice on how to deal with game playing. Waiting the right amount of time to return a call. Being strategically "busy" even when you're not. Making sure text messages have the air of mystery, not desperation—or, God forbid, actual interest.

I was seated next to Ophira Eisenberg, a stand-up comedian who had recently written a book about her adventures in dating, *Screw Everyone: Sleeping My Way to Monogamy*. (I've never gotten more comments from strangers while reading in public than I did with this brilliantly titled book.) Her response: That kind of sport sounded like great fun. When she was single she'd loved it. "No, I'm not giving you my number!" she'd reply if a man had been halfheartedly hitting on her. And suddenly he'd want her more.

At home that night, I realized Ophira's strategy was the only truly sane response to modern dating games. If you want to play, play! But know it's a game.

One of the things I've heard over and over again from couples describing what was different when they met "the One" was that for the first time, they didn't feel like they were in the middle of a romantic chess match. There was no guessing whether the other person was interested. They didn't worry about "the rules" on how long to wait before calling or setting up the next date. The whole thing felt relaxed and transparent, not fraught with the typical "Does he or she like me?" anxiety.

That's how it was with Aaron. When I texted him twenty minutes after the end of our first date, I didn't stay up all night doubting myself, like I usually would have. I never wondered if I would see him again or if he was into me. We didn't race into the relationship, but it was always clear that there would be a next date—and a next. And that was enough.

If you find yourself endlessly worrying about your next move or spending hours on the phone with friends, trying to decode your date's behavior, take that as a sign. You've found a partner for playing tag, but not for life.

Games are meant to be fun, so if you're in the midst of one and can find a way to enjoy it, then by all means, play on. Otherwise, forget it. You're better off at home with a glass of wine and a quick round of solitaire. At least that way you'll know when you've won.

Just Do It

Is there a particular someone you spend most of your waking hours thinking about? Someone who makes your palms sweat and stomach flip?

Maybe it's a best friend who knows you better than anyone in the world. Or a lovely stranger you see every day—same time, same place, same commuter bus route—but have never spoken to. Will you make a move? Please?

I'm sure it seems safer to keep things theoretical. That way you can't get hurt, or be disappointed by reality. I get it. All my high school romances took place entirely inside my head.

But if you want things to actually happen in your life—with this person or anyone else—you have to do *something*. Anything!

I've never met anyone who's had a more intense crush than Runy, a graphic designer who grew up in Zimbabwe. His first day on the job as a freelancer for a nonprofit organization, he met Junie, the effervescent daughter of Haitian immigrants, who was also new to the company. They laughed together about their rhyming names. He was immediately entranced: "She was so beautiful."

And then he didn't see her again. They worked on opposite schedules and after a few months she left for graduate school. But when she returned to the organization sixteen months later he was as struck by her as he had been the first time.

Runy, shy and quiet by nature, worked in the office just one day a week, and that one day a week he would say hello. It was all he could muster, though Junie was incessantly on his mind. He tried to convince himself that if he could just ignore his feelings, they would go away.

But, he told me, "It wasn't like any other crush I'd had. It was scary to like someone that much and not have talked to them."

Finally, after an office Christmas party, Runy, Junie, and a group of coworkers continued on to a club. The two danced all night, just as they had in Runy's dreams. But in the months that followed, he still couldn't figure out how to talk to her in the office.

Finally the torment became too much. He agonized and then made the call, leaving a voice mail inviting her to dinner. Junie had always thought he was nice, but she wasn't sure if he was asking her on a date. To be polite she said yes anyway.

It *was* a date, of course. He showed up with flowers and wine. They quickly connected over dinner, talking about their families and shared love of history. She told him she didn't think they should date—"the office is too small"—but by that point Runy had found his courage.

He sent her a bouquet for her birthday, called her every day, and even told her he was going to marry her one day. Her guard began to come down and by the time she left for a long weekend a month later, she knew she was in love. Two long years after they had first met, Runy's affection was finally mutual.

But it never would have come to fruition if he hadn't picked up the phone. Other people I interviewed told me they sat on their feelings until a dream forced them to make a move—or until they were sure they'd burst if they didn't say something.

It's risky, I know. Taking action feels like the most frightening thing you can imagine doing. And a negative response—rejection or the loss of a close friend—seems like more than you can bear. But the risks of doing nothing—of not giving yourself the chance to find out if you could have what Runy and Junie have—are greater.

And if you put yourself out there and the response is "No, thanks," then you'll have to trust that it wasn't meant to be. And that you're now freed for whatever better option the universe has been concocting for you.

Regardless of the outcome, there will be solace in knowing that you tried. You won't have to spend the rest of your life wondering "What if?" You'll know that you were brave enough to give yourself—and love—a chance.

Make a Wish

During dinner at one wedding, I wandered into the garden of the old mansion where the event was being held. There I found the couple's three-year-old son playing by a big stone fountain.

I gave the boy a penny and told him to make a wish. After he tossed it in the fountain, he turned back to me and beamed. "I wished for cake!" he exclaimed.

About half an hour later, his two fathers cut their beautiful cake and gave the boy a slice.

I tell you this story simply as proof that sometimes wishes really do come true.

Put It Out There

My first Halloween as a wedding reporter I found myself sitting on a rural Maryland hilltop, surrounded by wizards, knights, and angels of death. The sky was ashen and a strong gust of wind blew a broomstick from its place atop a makeshift altar. The chilling theme from *Edward Scissorhands* played as the bride made her way down the aisle.

Normally, to blend in, I wear a simple black dress to weddings. So I'd panicked when I woke up that day and remembered that everyone at this wedding would be in costume. I spent the morning running between Halloween stores and secondhand shops, trying to quickly pull together a disguise. Sitting on that grassy knoll, looking like a disheveled Judy Jetson, all I could think was, "Am I even still a journalist? I don't think Bob Woodward did this; this was not Joan Didion's path."

Of course, it turned out to be fascinating and fun. Woodward and Didion missed out. In all their illustrious years in journalism, did they ever get to see a table laid with food and wine, reserved for the deceased? Or watch a horror-movie host named Count Gore de Vol hypnotize wedding guests? I don't think so.

I may not have left that wedding fully convinced of the existence of magic, but I was certainly a believer in the power of intentions.

The bride and groom, Christina and Daniel, first met as children. At thirteen, she confessed a budding crush to her diary, but they lost track of each other when her family moved to a different nearby town. She was a Goth teenager five years later, when he walked into the video store where she was working.

"Cool hair," she said, nodding at his orange Mohawk.

They quickly became a couple and struggled through early adulthood together. He worked a forklift at a steel mill while she went to college and found odd jobs to pay the bills.

Along the way Daniel became interested in paganism, a spiritual belief system that seeks harmony with nature. He found a mentor and delved into the faith. Christina was interested and accepting, but held on to aspects of the religion in which she was raised, coming to consider herself a "Catholic witch." (But then, don't we all?)

The pair lived in a ratty apartment in Baltimore, walking

by drug dealers and gangbangers every time they went to the corner market. They dreamed of getting married but couldn't afford a wedding. Frustrated and desperate, Daniel began casting spells for money and prosperity. Christina prayed that God would lift them from poverty.

One Thursday, at the mill, Daniel's coworkers laughed as he told them the request he'd put out to the universe: "I don't care who wins the lottery, as long as it's somebody near me." Two days later he fell asleep on his couch, the television still on, after drinking a bit too much ale at the local Renaissance fair. When he woke up, Daniel couldn't believe what he saw on the screen: There was his pagan mentor, accepting a giant lottery check for $48 million. Daniel's newly wealthy friend bought the couple a house, employed them both as personal assistants, and then funded and presided over their Halloween wedding—the one they'd always dreamed about.

I'm not suggesting we all go check out witchcraft books from the local library. I don't even want to get all "law of attraction"-ish on you—and obviously Daniel and Christina are an extreme example anyway—but I will say that I'm constantly amazed at how often I've spoken to people who articulated their desire for lasting love to some higher power and then felt that their wish was granted.

One woman, nearing forty and fearing her chances for a long, loving marriage were growing slim, slipped into church during her lunch hour, lit a candle, and fervently prayed that God would help her find "the one." Later that week she sat staring at the online profile of the man who would eventually become her husband.

Others wrote lists of the essential qualities they were looking for in a mate and slept with them under the bed. Some asked friends and relatives not just to set them up, but to pray for their romantic future. One woman credits her grandmother's invocation of St. Anthony with her success in finding a husband. Another recalls being surprised when, the day after telling her mother that she was fully ready to settle down, her best male friend suggested they date. "I was really scared," she told me. "My prayers had never been answered so quickly."

I don't know why this stuff happens. It could be that when people put their wishes out into the world—and believe they'll be heard—they start to walk more confidently through life. Or it could just be coincidence.

But either way, there's nothing to lose. If there's something you want, why not ask your favorite all-powerful being—God, perhaps, or the universe, or Oprah—for a little help?

Maybe you waste your breath. Or maybe your best friend wins the lottery and you find your soul mate. If you do, let me know. I'll unpack my Judy Jetson costume and come to the wedding.

Give Nice a Chance

For a while, part of my job was to find guests to answer readers' anonymous relationship questions in a weekly online chat.

Usually these hour-long sessions left me disconsolate. Good Lord, the suffering—it was too much. Despondent outcries poured onto the screen faster than I could read. People in relationships were disappointed, lonely, and miserable—and often longing to be free. Single people were disappointed, lonely, and miserable—and, of course, desperate to be in a relationship.

An example: *"I never had love. And now fear I never will. The 'love of my life' dumped me and married someone else. I married (now I realize) out of fear of being alone at forty-three. Now I'm fifty and fear it's too late to EVER know reciprocal love in my life and it makes me sad and jealous and mad."*

Got any words of wisdom for this gal? Have at it.

Each week was a reminder of how difficult intimate relationships often are—and how vital they are to our basic well-being.

One week I invited a well-regarded psychologist, who had recently published a new book on love, to host a chat. But as I watched his responses to readers' questions appear on my screen I grew increasingly frustrated. People asked about what to look for in a mate, how to know when they'd found the right person, and how to trust again after a betrayal. The psychologist's answers were like a broken record. His message: "Choose someone kind. Choose someone kind. Choose someone kind. *Be* kind, and choose someone kind."

"Well, duh?" I thought. No one sets out to marry an egomaniacal asshole. Most people don't dream of ending up with cruel, controlling partners.

And yet . . .

One Friday night I was walking home from happy hour on a bustling D.C. street when I saw a man punch his girlfriend in the face. Twice. It was a shocking, horrifying thing to witness. As I approached the woman to see if she was okay, she looked at me with tears rolling down her swollen face and said, "He saw a number in my phone. He thinks it's another guy, but it's not like that."

Soon cops had the man in shackles. I was heartbroken for the woman, but relieved that for the moment she was safe. Then, a couple of months later, I got a court summons to testify against the man.

The woman sat on the other side of the courtroom. She was beautiful, with round, full cheeks and long eyelashes. We both watched as the man was escorted in, wearing an orange jumpsuit. I answered the lawyers' questions about what I had seen. Then it was the woman's turn. She got on the stand and said that the incident had never happened.

He was found guilty anyway, but before the man was sentenced, the woman had a chance to speak directly to the judge. "You don't understand," she pleaded. "That's my fiancé. We were gonna get married."

As extreme as that example is, we all know someone who picked an unkind partner. I've seen it, sometimes, in couples I've interviewed. When one person continually interrupts or dismisses or criticizes what the other was saying. And this happens, remember, in conversations about why the two are in love!

No one sets out to fall for a jerk, but we too often easily ignore the warning signs. I know *I* dated guys my friends and family didn't love—not because they were abusive, but because they didn't make me a priority and weren't really there when I needed them.

It happens. You fall for someone's charms and then ignore how mean they are to waitresses or how they brush off your young niece—or how your dog, who loves everyone, growls whenever they come around. "Choose someone kind" is not the worst mantra to keep in mind as you date. And it could certainly save some tears down the road.

One bride I met, a whip-smart lawyer named Debbi, spent most of her twenties dating attractive, exciting, not particularly kind guys. When she met a soft-spoken doctor named Art at a wedding, she wasn't immediately taken with him. She agreed to a date and enjoyed his company but discovered on subsequent meetings that Art was the kind of guy who orders the same dish every time he visits a restaurant. He was steady, reliable, and not exactly living on the edge.

When he moved away for a residency, he wanted to stay together, but she didn't think their connection was strong enough to survive the distance. They kept in touch over the next few years, Art always hoping the romance would be rekindled. "We were very compatible," he told me. "I was just happy when I was with her."

But Debbi still wasn't sure. It wasn't until she described Art's sweet, steadfast nature to a friend that something clicked.

"'You know, you marry the nice guy,'" Debbi recalled her friend saying. "It was like a foreign concept to me. I was like, 'No. I didn't know that.' So many of these guys I've dated, I would never want them to be, like, the father of my children."

Of course, today Art is the doting father of their young son.

I loved the way a woman named Lynne put it just before her second wedding. She was a fifty-seven-year-old who'd married for the first time in her mid-thirties. After thirteen months of marriage, her husband, a foreign service officer whom she adored, died of a rare blood cancer.

To honor him, Lynne joined the foreign service herself and served as a diplomat in Cairo, Brussels, and Casablanca. Along the way she dated—and even got engaged once—but never married. Lynne had been fully loved by a wonderful man once before, and she wasn't going to settle for anything less. She was waiting, she told me, "for somebody who's really *good*. The quality of goodness, I think, is highly underrated." And without it, she decided, no one was worth the trouble.

Lynne was working at the American embassy in Paris when she met a fellow diplomat named Jud. She was impressed by how well his reports were written and how respectfully he treated the younger staffers. When he took her boating on the Seine he told her he was a divorced father of three who hadn't dated much. As their relationship progressed she found out he liked to fix cars, write poetry, and wander through art museums. She discovered he was clearheaded and unflappable— qualities that proved useful when the two served together in Haiti during the 2010 earthquake. Through everything, she found him to be wholly, transparently good.

"I knew what I needed," she said before her wedding to Jud. "And I was willing to hold out for it."

Just Be Yourself

Rebecca was a contortionist. In one relationship after another she'd adjust her own personality to fit that of her boyfriend. She'd adapt, tweak, or bury portions of herself in the name of keeping the peace—and the guy. But each time she suppressed her quirks, or took on a boyfriend's interests as her own, the results were the same. "Inevitably I'd go, 'I can't do this anymore,'" she recalls. And then it was over.

Shakespeare and the grandmothers of the world are in consensus on this one. "To thine own self be true." Or, "Just be yourself, honey!"

But, you might say, what if the person you're dating is *perfect* for you, and everything is wonderful and amazing and glorious—just as long as you remember to keep your voice down, because even though you're a naturally loud person, they can't stand anything above a whisper? Or they insist on you becoming a stay-at-home parent when your career is deeply fulfilling? Or your real passions are cross-dressing and Civil War reenactments—activities they deride?

That's not such a big deal, perhaps, until suddenly it is. Until the day you wake up and realize you cannot go another moment whispering at home with the kids instead of cross-dressing at a Civil War reenactment.

The façade always cracks. A secret: At the beginning of relationships, everyone pretends they don't have the physical capacity to fart. And then, one day, a little something sneaks out. And hopefully—healthfully—before too long it all starts to, uh, flow.

Because it cannot be contained forever. You will burst. And there's a similar sense of compounded agony when you deny some fundamental part of yourself.

We could avoid reams of heartaches if we were all confident enough to be fully ourselves right from the start—failings, idiosyncrasies, and all. It's just not that easy. It means occasionally overriding the abiding desire to be liked and accepted. But if someone only likes the paler, polished version of you, how can you trust that they really like you at all? They don't even know you.

If you don't believe Grandma or Shakespeare, listen to Amy Brunell. She's an Ohio State University psychology professor who has studied the impact of authenticity in close relationships.

Brunell and her colleagues found that when people were true to themselves they experienced a range of psychological benefits. They had higher self-esteem, were more satisfied with life, and struggled less with depression. And people who were more fully themselves in the context of their romantic relationships felt better supported and validated by their partners.

Back to Rebecca: She was thirty when she decided she wasn't going to pretend anymore. Doctors blamed her frequent tension headaches on stress from studying for the bar exam, but in her quiet, solitary moments, she knew that wasn't the real cause. The man she was dating wanted to marry and all she could think was, "Well, I guess that's what settling down means—you settle." And lose part of yourself along the way.

Finally, she decided she wasn't going to do it. She would never again hide a portion of herself—her big laugh, her penchant for dirty humor—for this or any other guy. She'd rather be single forever.

To take her mind off things, she flew to Utah for a solo week at ski school. She immediately noticed her handsome Spanish ski instructor, Marco, and felt a little shy around him at first. But once she was sure he wasn't interested, she let loose, cracking jokes to make the other students laugh. At the end of the week Marco invited Rebecca to go swimming, pulled her close in the water, and kissed her.

She extended her vacation by five days and planned a return trip to the mountains a few months later. Marco, who'd spent a decade crossing continents as a ski instructor, enrolled in an MBA program and the two made a life together in Colorado. They married in Washington, D.C., where she'd grown up. Their wedding occurred, appropriately enough, in the midst of a wild snowstorm.

"I never thought I'd be lucky enough to find my soul mate," Rebecca told me the day before the wedding. "I thought that was just something people say."

Maybe it wasn't simply luck that led her to that moment. Maybe it was the courage she found to let the world—and Marco—see her for who she was.

The Most Important Word

I was once asked to talk to an undergraduate journalism class.

I always feel like a fraud doing stuff like this, and am usually tempted to scrap the lecture and lead a parade to the nearest dive bar to show off my flip-cup skills. So as I stood there, faking my way through the guest spot, I asked a question of my audience: "What do you think is the one word I hear most often when people explain why they chose the person they did to spend the rest of their life with?"

The guessing went on forever. Or at least until the professor looked at her watch and asked me to move it along. Love? Trust? Laughter? Chemistry? No. No. Nope. No. The word, I told them, was *comfortable*. Seventy to 80 percent of the couples I interview talk about how comfortable they feel with each other. Often they use the word and then immediately apologize. "That sounds terrible," they'll say. "It sounds like settling."

But they don't mean it like that. Lisa, a single mom in her thirties, took a gamble when she got on a Charlotte, North Carolina–bound plane with her young son to visit a man she'd never met. She and Leland had attended the same veterinary school and had friends in common but didn't connect until years after graduation. By then they were both divorced parents. After becoming friends on Facebook, they started to chat online and then on the phone.

But Lisa was still wary when Leland offered to host her and her son for a Carolina Panthers game. Her boy, however, was a raving Panthers fan—almost as devoted as Leland, who had a room in his house dedicated to the team—so she decided it was worth the risk.

Leland picked Lisa and her son up at the airport and immediately, she said, it felt "comfortable," a word she used five times over the course of our two-hour interview. "It wasn't forced or awkward—it was as if we'd always known each other." Within eight months, Leland moved to Maryland and the two were married.

Comfort is not what we're taught to seek in romantic relationships. We look for sparks, chemistry, desire, and an immediate sense of knowing. How did Danny and Sandy identify "the one that they want" in *Grease*? It was through chills that were multiplying and power, electrifying. God knows you don't squeeze into your best black spandex just to feel like you're cozied up on a Barcalounger.

Hollywood and romance novels can't do comfortable: We'd

fall asleep. Can you imagine a movie where two people meet, feel at ease with each other, and then mutually agree to transition into a committed relationship? Blech. I got bored just writing that sentence. We want our love stories full of rapture, pain, and passion. Couples torn apart by fate are good. So are smart-ass rivals who despise each other and trade witty jabs before falling into the sack together.

Society doesn't tell us to seek a mate who embodies the qualities of a good pair of pajamas: soft and warm, but loose enough to really let you breathe. In the end, though, isn't that what we need? A companion with whom we can be our whole, unkempt, awkward, imperfect, occasionally appalling selves? Someone around whom we're not sucking in our stomach or walking on eggshells or bracing for judgment?

I think comfortable is what most people eventually choose, even if it's not what they're seeking at the start of their dating adventures. I've heard the word so often that I eventually began to worry about couples who don't use it, or a synonym— *easy, effortless, natural.*

A buddy of mine once admitted that he wasn't able to be himself around his longtime girlfriend as much as he was with our group of friends. But that was a good thing, he insisted, because it forced him to be "better" with her. I saw his point, but how long can that last? How long can a person monitor their behavior before they start to crack? Or seek an outlet elsewhere?

A few years ago, a twenty-something colleague mentioned she was looking for a man who challenged her. My wise friend Scott, who's been with the same man for decades, just shook his head. "Isn't life challenging enough already?" he asked. "Don't you want to come home to a soft place where you can just take a break?"

The first time Aaron and I went out for drinks, we sat together for more than five hours. Sure, it helped that there was a special on Miller Lite bottles. But the real draw was the conversation. It was just so fun and easy. Time seemed to evaporate. And it continued to feel that way in the weeks and months that followed.

It's not that there wasn't excited anticipation and pre-date jitters and those all-important sparks. Those things were there, but they were accompanied by an underlying sense of calm. I never felt self-conscious. I wasn't secretly clenching my stomach muscles in his presence, the way I had in previous relationships.

With Aaron, I understood why comfortable was so important. It made everything easier—the talking and silence, the laughing and fighting, the intimacy and occasional tears. I didn't have to hold anything back. So I felt fully known. And then, because of that, fully loved.

I wondered what would happen when the students in the class I was visiting went out to the bars that night. Would they be on the lookout for somebody who was not just cute and exciting, but also made them feel comfortable? I doubt it. Everyone has to put in some time waiting for lightning to strike before realizing it's not much fun to get burned. But maybe one day they'll think back and remember: Life is hard. Find someone easy.

Same Difference

I didn't intend to like Neil Warren, the founder of eHarmony. From what I'd read, our politics were a bit different. But after an hour in his presence, I wanted him to adopt me as a long-lost grandchild—and not just so I could swim in his pools of online matchmaking money.

Warren was every bit as warm and hokey—and likable—as he appeared on television. Seated next to his elegant, silver-haired wife in a hotel dining room, he spoke in slow, meandering monologues, interrupting himself only to see if I needed anything to eat or drink.

He was in Washington, D.C., for a media tour and he wanted me to know about all the satisfied couples who regularly sent him wedding pictures and holiday cards. And about how the site's algorithm for romance—which pairs up people who have similar characteristics—was the key to a satisfying marriage.

I nodded a lot and listened attentively. At the end of the conversation, he opened his arms to hug me. I never wrote a story about the interview, but he was, I had to admit, a very sweet man.

So sweet, in fact, that I didn't have the heart to tell him I didn't buy what he was selling. At least not fully. Yes, eHarmony has been undeniably successful in bringing together a pool of commitment-minded singles who might not otherwise meet. But I just can't get behind the company's fundamental premise that similarity between partners is the most important element of a good relationship.

Every time I interview a couple, I end with this question: "You're choosing each other out of all the people in the world—at least theoretically—so what do you think it is that makes your relationship work? What makes it tick?"

Some couples look at me with blank stares and open mouths. Those ones I worry about. The rest usually talk about how their personalities *just fit.*

And then they elaborate—demonstrating that a "good fit" can mean two very different things.

Half the couples will explain that they are truly opposites in almost every regard—he's outgoing, she's an introvert; he's logical, she's creative—and because of that they fill each other's gaps. "His strengths are my weaknesses," they often say. "And vice versa. So we're better together than we are on our own."

One of my favorites from this camp was a couple named

Jason and Jocelyn. When they met he was a straight-laced NFL lineman who liked to spend his free time at home and planned on going to business school when his football career ended. She was an artistic, free-spirited medical student who wore her hair in long dreadlocks and dragged him to every interesting restaurant and outdoor festival she could find. They fell in love and started referring to themselves as "the black Dharma and Greg." (They will both note, however, that it was Jason who uncharacteristically forgot to update his passport before their destination wedding in Jamaica, forcing Jocelyn and their fifty guests to spend a week in paradise without him. To make up for it, he single-handedly planned a do-over wedding in Baltimore. Tip: When throwing a destination wedding, make sure you are legally allowed to board the plane to get there.)

The *other* half of couples I interview will tell me how much they are alike. "It's almost uncanny," they'll say. "We were raised in similar families, have similar viewpoints, personalities, and taste in music and movies. We can almost always complete each other's sentences." It makes sense, of course, that people who belong to the same religion or who are both vegetarians have a natural affinity and less to argue about. But it goes beyond that: More than once people have said something like "She's the girl me" or "He's the male version of me." It always makes me think of the *Seinfeld* episode where Jerry dates Janeane Garafalo. "She's just like me!" Jerry exclaims. "She talks like me. She acts like me. She even orders cereal in a restaurant. We even have the same initials. Wait a minute, I just realized what's going on. Now I know what I've been looking for all these years—myself!"

I bet Neil Warren was bummed it didn't work out between Jerry and Janeane. But Portia Dyrenforth wouldn't have been surprised. Dyrenforth is a psychology professor at Hobart and William Smith Colleges who has studied compatibility in couples. At the start of every semester, she asks her class if they think couples who are similar are more likely to be happy. Her students usually nod in unison. Then she asks if they know couples who are very different but seem happy together. They nod again. As a society, Dyrenforth says, we've been led to believe that "birds of a feather flock together." But we also know that "opposites attract."

To find out which is really more accurate, Dyrenforth examined the personality traits of more than 11,600 couples. She wanted to see if their similarity in characteristics like openness, extroversion, conscientiousness, and agreeableness correlated with higher rates of marital satisfaction. But no: Similarity neither hurt nor benefited the relationship, although she did find that people whose partners were agreeable, conscientious, and emotionally stable were likely to be happy with their relationships and life in general. (Because, as previously discussed, being with a grumpy, unreliable nutjob doesn't usually spell long-term domestic bliss.)

The lesson: Date someone who is just like you—or don't. It won't really matter as long as you've found a good fit.

Don't Look for Lightning

It would be nice if God arranged for a choir of angels to sing at the precise moment when you meet the love of your life. That would add some appropriate theatrics to the occasion, but it would also offer an important sense of confirmation. Like on the first day of the semester when your professor would announce the name of the class, just to clear out lost souls who'd wandered into the wrong room.

After all, we expect *something* to happen when *it* finally happens.

I interviewed a few people who described the moment they met their future spouse as magical: intense eye contact across a room, a jolt surging through their body, or seeing the object of their desire bathed in a strange light. But these were by far the minority . . . and there was almost always a good deal of alcohol involved.

For most couples it was much less electrifying. Sometimes

one would consider the other attractive and develop a crush over time. More often they found as they spent time together—either on dates or in the office or around their apartment complex—that they just liked the other's company.

Toward the end of my first year of writing about weddings I sat down with a couple named Mara and John. Mara's government coworkers had invited her to a party to meet a single friend. Meanwhile, they'd told John they knew a girl who was looking for a one-night stand, which Mara certainly was not. Mara was in the middle of moving to a new apartment on the day of the party, so she showed up late and in a bad mood, a condition that worsened as she felt people looking at the two of them, waiting to see what would happen.

John sensed her annoyance, but, he told me, "there was something about her that really intrigued me." He got her number, called, and convinced her to go to dinner. Mara was logical, organized, and hardworking; John was long-haired, fun-loving, and spontaneous. But there was an ease between them that led to more dates.

Soon they were having dinner on the twelfth of every month to mark their anniversary—which they continued to do for *twelve years* before he finally proposed. John knew so many people who'd been divorced, he worried that getting married would only mess up the good thing they had. Mara felt silly calling him her boyfriend after all that time and wanted to make it official. It wasn't until he walked Mara down the aisle at his brother's wedding that John decided this was what he wanted, too.

They'd been together for 147 months by the time I met them at a Starbucks a few days before the wedding. John was steeling himself to cut off his ponytail in order to look dapper for the big day.

As we wrapped up the interview, Mara asked if I was married. This was several months after my breakup. "Not yet," I said, shutting off my tape recorder and putting on my winter coat. Couples often wanted to know about my personal life after revealing the intimate details of their own. I couldn't help but feel embarrassed that I was single and positioned as this supposed wedding guru, though I'd never come close to having a wedding of my own.

But I didn't want her to be sad for me, so I told her something true: that covering weddings had actually made me more optimistic, because I got to meet with couples like her and John, who made me realize that love happens all the time, in all kinds of ways.

"Yes," she said as we walked out the door. "And it doesn't have to be a thunderbolt. It can be this calm, steady reassurance. I wish that for you."

I was so struck by Mara's sensitivity and kindness—and by the reminder of how much I wanted the kind of bond they had—that I got into my car and cried.

I never forgot Mara's wish for me. And I wish the same for you.

COMMITMENT

When Aaron and I began dating, we lived four and a half blocks apart. This situation was ideal—we were close enough to walk to each other's apartments at night, but far enough that we frequented different drugstores and never ran into each other buying toilet paper or tampons.

By the time we decided to live together, we'd each spent several years in our own cozy apartments—and neither of us wanted to leave. He loved his little nook with the fireplace and in-unit laundry; I preferred my third-story hacienda with the fire escape and deep tub.

After countless back-and-forths, we did the only reasonable thing—we moved to a new place exactly in the middle. The point of the story is this: Change is hard. Compromise is messy. Also, proximity is the secret agent of romance. We might not have made it as a couple if we'd had to get on a subway to see each other.

When you're dating, you assume you're going through the hard part—trying to find the right person, riding a roller coaster of expectations, and grappling with the anguish of uncertainty. You never consider *that there's another hard part right around the corner—transitioning from being an independent operator to being part of a two-person unit. When "your life" becomes "our life" and everything you have—time, money, energy, priorities—is suddenly shared.*

At the beginning of a relationship you get to be hopelessly in love, desperate to spend every minute together, yet able to return to your separate quarters and cut your toenails in private. You spend enough time apart that you actually miss each other, instead of being annoyed that your darling beloved is still here. It's alone time, really, that's wasted on the young.

But commitment, when you start planning a shared future and figuring out how to get there, is also exciting. All of a sudden, it's decision time. Is this really the person with whom you want to live out your days? Where will the two of you reside? How many rescue animals will be invited along for the ride?

It's all very adult. And a little bit scary. As Eat, Pray, Love *author Elizabeth Gilbert wrote in her follow-up book,* Committed: A Skeptic Makes Peace with Marriage, *"There is no choice more intensely personal, after all, than whom you choose to marry; that choice tells us, to a large extent, who you are." And in time that choice shapes who you are, as you blend your lives and hopes and dreams and opinions on appropriate shower curtain colors.*

We don't get to move from puppy love straight to the golden years of a decades-old marriage, where every joke and wrinkle is a testament to the enduring strength of your bond. First we have to really learn each other. And, in doing so, we have the opportunity to learn about ourselves in the context of that most wonderful, enriching, confounding entity: a committed relationship.

It's not always as dreamy or exhilarating as falling in love. But this stage isn't about champagne and sweet nothings; it's about bricks and mortar. The idea is to build a solid foundation for your love—hopefully one that will serve you for many years to come.

Who's Ready?

If you're of my generation, you probably learned a lot of important life lessons from the classic nineties sitcom *Family Matters*. Maybe you learned that families should always stick together. Or that it's important to be nice to nerds because when you take away the glasses and pocket protectors, they're all secretly hot. Or that, in the end, there are few problems in life that can't be solved with a jelly doughnut. (Thanks, Carl Winslow.)

At least, those were my big takeaways as a kid. Then, a couple of decades later, one *Family Matters* cast member taught me that when it comes to finding a spouse, people have to be ready. And by "people," I mean men.

I was a women's studies minor and I consider myself a feminist. So I know the dangers of generalizing. And, to be sure, in my years on the weddings beat I encountered plenty of women who were skittish of commitment and others who

were smart enough to know they needed time to mature before sharing their lives with a partner.

But I met many more women who felt they'd been ready
for a serious, lasting relationship for years and just could not
find the right partner. And I met an outsized number of men
who, for one reason or another, just weren't prepared to tie
their life to one person—until, suddenly, they were.

This was never more clear to me than the day I sat down
with the woman who played Steve Urkel's enduring crush,
Laura Winslow. Her real name is Kellie Williams and she is
lovely—smart, funny, self-aware, and honest. After the show
went off the air Williams returned to the D.C. area, where she
was born, and set up an arts organization for kids.

It was two weeks before their wedding when Kellie and her
fiancé, Hannibal, told me their story. For years Hannibal Jack-
son, a government contracting executive, had been an enthu-
siastic bachelor, juggling multiple women and a packed
schedule of nights on the town.

But after accompanying a coworker to church in his late
twenties, he began taking his faith seriously. And after several
more years of chasing girls, he woke up one morning and decided he was ready to marry.

"Can you believe that?" Kellie said indignantly, shaking
her head after Hannibal explained his thought process. She
knew so many women who'd put in years—decades!—trying
to find a husband. They'd spent countless dollars on match-

makers, dating sites, and consolation pints of ice cream. And a guy just has to *decide* it's time?

Of course it wasn't quite that simple. For months Hannibal prayed for a woman "after God's own heart." When first introduced to Kellie, he wasn't all that impressed with her Hollywood ties; as a teen he'd been too busy spending Friday nights at the mall to watch her show. But a mutual friend had been trying to set up the two for years, so Hannibal asked for Kellie's number and invited her out for a jog. Within a few dates he was enchanted by her energy and creative spirit.

And after two weeks, Kellie—who wasn't going to allow herself to get screwed around—laid down an ultimatum: "You're either my boyfriend, or this is the last time we're going to talk." The next move was his. Of course, Hannibal chose option number one, and then, after ten months of dating, he proposed.

It's impossible to say what would have happened had Kellie and Hannibal met a decade earlier. Perhaps they would have felt a spark of connection that couldn't ignite because they were at different places in life, looking for different things.

They say timing is everything. Whoever "they" are, they have a point. If a person ready for a picket fence and minivan falls for someone who still loves playing the field, they'll likely end up frustrated at best. Heartbroken at worst.

Because you can't make someone be ready. Each of us goes through life in our own way, at our own pace. Some are born ready to settle down and push baby carriages. Others happily eschew that kind of domesticity their whole lives. Another contingent are happy to be with one person but dislike the idea of a legally binding marriage.

Even people in relationships need the freedom to move toward commitment at a rate that feels comfortable to them. I have always run ahead of schedule with Aaron. I said "I love you" first and was routinely eager to move to the next step— cohabitation, engagement, marriage—six months before he was. Our mismatched timelines annoyed both of us on occasion, but we just had to be patient with each other and make sure we agreed on the ultimate destination.

Patience is a necessary virtue. But that doesn't mean you should assume that someone with fundamentally different desires will wind up on the same page as you. All you can do is give the situation a clear-eyed evaluation to decide whether it truly feels right at this point, and how likely it seems your partner will eventually want what you want.

Then you just have trust that if it's meant to be, everything will work out when the timing is right—for both of you.

The Long and Winding Road

One of the first brides I interviewed described the story of her romance as "part fairy tale, part *Jerry Springer* episode." I loved her immediately.

Most people aren't that honest with themselves, never mind a newspaper reporter who intends to put all the details of their personal life in print. We want our love stories to be sweet, simple, and tidy. But it's rarely that clean—and when it is, it doesn't stay that way for long. Human existence is complicated. And Kerilyn knew that.

She first met Peter as an undergraduate at West Virginia University. Kerilyn was a free-spirited extrovert with plans to transfer to a design school in Georgia. Peter pursued her anyway, and helped her pack on the day she left.

"I knew she was leaving and I knew it wasn't really going to work out," Peter told me. "But it was like, 'I really like her.' I like her smile, her face. I was just attracted to her."

They didn't keep in touch during the three years she studied interior design and he trained to become a chef. But when a mutual friend mentioned Peter's name after they'd both graduated, Kerilyn decided to call from Washington, D.C., and see if he was heading to the WVU homecoming game. As soon as he heard her voice, Peter, then living in New Jersey, chose to go. "I always thought about her," he remembered. "When she called me and told me she was going to go, I was ecstatic."

Back on their old stomping grounds, Peter found himself enamored once again—only this time it was mutual. "It was a real connection," said Kerilyn, who speaks as if she can't get the words out fast enough.

For a year, they dated long-distance; then Peter relocated to be with her. He was buoyed by her spontaneity and ebullience; she was calmed by his steadiness and wry humor. But soon they broke up. Peter worked insane hours at a restaurant. Kerilyn was stressed about the trajectory of her career. The fighting became too much.

Even when they weren't officially "together," however, they were constantly together. "We loved each other and we were on-and-off. I would spend nights at his place, but we weren't officially dating," Kerilyn said. "This went on for three years."

Eventually she wanted more. But when she was ready to commit, Peter wasn't, so she decided she had to move on. "The timing was off," she said. "I knew that once he was ready, he'd come looking for me, but I just couldn't wait."

Of course, as soon as Kerilyn was gone, Peter realized what he'd lost. And he was certain he could get it back. "She was in a relationship, but that didn't matter to me," he recalled. "Because I knew I was going to marry her. I knew we loved each other and I knew it was going to happen."

Kerilyn harshly tried to convince him otherwise. She never stopped loving Peter but felt that her new boyfriend deserved a chance. She told Peter to stop calling, texting, and emailing. He finally got the picture. But there was something missing in Kerilyn's relationship. She was lonely. And her sister, who'd stayed in touch with Peter, knew it. She arranged a meeting between the two.

By then Peter was also dating someone else, but when he and Kerilyn met up at a riverside park, the two knew what was going to happen. There were tears and hugs and lengthy explanations. Two months later they were engaged.

My favorite couples to write about often have roller-coaster stories like that one. They've experienced challenges—and doubts and roadblocks—and still chosen each other. They don't expect perfection, because they already know it doesn't exist. And they want a life together anyway.

Often one or both people need time to grow and develop before they're really ready to commit. Sometimes it takes the threat of losing each other before they realize what they have. One couple I wrote about was on-again, off-again for years, until she was diagnosed with stage-four cancer. From that moment on, he never left her side. Today she's in remission and they're married, with a small child. Their path to the altar wasn't straight, but by the time they got there, they'd already lived their vows: "for better or for worse, in sickness and in health."

Perhaps it'd be better if we were all a little more like Kerilyn and Peter. We could give up the guise of seamless perfection and be honest about the fact that we've caused our partners both great pleasure and great pain. It can be no other way. And the triumph is having stuck together through all of it.

As Kerilyn told me the week before her wedding, "It's such a crazy story. With on-ramps and off-ramps and detours. But in the end it's a fairy tale." Life with Peter, she said, was always "meant to be."

Express Yourself

One couple I interviewed hit a rough patch early on in their relationship. They'd always been intensely drawn to each other and were deeply in love, but it seemed that every few days they'd have a fight that threatened to derail everything.

Usually he would say or do something to upset her. Occasionally it was what he *failed* to say or do that set her off. She'd become quiet and withdrawn and when he asked what was wrong she'd almost always sullenly respond, "Nothing."

Exasperated, he finally lost it. "I'm a guy!" he cried. "We're idiots! You have to actually *tell* me what you want!" And guess what? When she did, things started to go a lot smoother.

Expressing our needs is not always easy and often doesn't come naturally, to men or to women. Maybe we resent having to do it at all. We'd prefer for our partner to understand us so intuitively that we never have to vocalize our needs. But unless you've shacked up with a professional psychic, it's probably best to pipe up about whatever it is you want. Then at least your partner has a *chance* of giving it to you.

Do you want to reserve morning conversations until you've had a cup of coffee and begun to feel human again? Explain that, rather than barking at the chipper early bird across the table. Do you expect to receive a kiss every time you walk in the house? Mention it, instead of stewing when you don't get one. In his wildly popular bestseller *The Five Love Languages: How to Express Heartfelt Commitment to Your Mate,* author Gary Chapman writes about the different methods people use to express and receive love. Some folks, for instance, feel most treasured when they're showered with gifts. Others place a premium on quality time spent with their partners. And while one man might prize physical affection, another might value loving words or acts, like a spouse picking up the dry cleaning or packing lunch.

Most of us wouldn't mind being treated to all those kindnesses, but Chapman says people usually prefer one method above the rest. The problem is that we often express love using the method *we* most prefer, not necessarily the one that means the most to our partner. It's not enough to treat others how you would like to be treated; treat them the way *they* want to be treated.

So if a person who needs to spend a lot of time with their partner to feel truly loved falls for someone who is always at the office—even if he never forgets to bring home flowers and chocolates—there's going to be friction. And the hardworking chocolate buyer probably won't understand why his beloved is always so angry or why he never receives any treats in return.

Obviously it takes self-awareness to know what we want in a relationship. It also takes courage to speak up about it and trust that our partner is open to listening. But it's a sign you may have found a keeper when you feel comfortable talking about your needs and value the relationship enough to express them.

I was in awe of a young bride named Abby the minute I met her. By the time she was twenty-five she'd earned a master's degree in social work and purchased her own home, where we talked. She had a garden growing out back, a candle burning on the dining room table, and a crisp white shirt that looked perfectly tailored to her petite frame.

Bill had been similarly stunned by Abby when she showed up at his sister's engagement party a few years earlier, although his heart dropped once he learned she had a boyfriend. But when that relationship fizzled, Bill's sister helped arrange a date between the two.

Even at that first dinner together, he felt like he could open up to her in a way he'd never been able to with other women. Within months, both were sure this relationship was it. They decided to move in together less than a year later, but before Bill packed his bags, Abby asked that they both write down a list of expectations.

"It was really, really detailed stuff," she told me. "Like, 'If you come home from work and you've had a bad day, where are you going to go in the house? And how am I going to know that you need some space?' I think couples expect these things, but they don't let the other person know."

Maybe we should all be required to get graduate degrees in social work before we're allowed to date. I couldn't believe how wise—and totally logical—Abby's idea was.

It's worth taking a page from her book. Ask questions: What does the ideal division of household chores look like to you? How much alone time do you need each day? What are your thoughts about combining finances?

And speak up about what you want. It doesn't guarantee you'll get exactly what you're after, but if your partner is the person you think they are, they'll at least try to meet your needs. It might not come naturally to them. You may need to ask a thousand times and accept that sometimes things won't go your way. But the good ones will listen, work to understand, and make an effort.

You just have to give them the chance.

Love Is Not All You Need

My favorite quote from a political figure probably won't make it into the history books. Seated on a couch next to her husband during a television interview, Michelle Obama matter-of-factly explained, "I like Barack. I don't just love him. I *like* him. I like who he is."

That might not seem like the most romantic statement of all time. But after more than twenty years, two kids, and countless campaign stops, she likes the man. Still!

Honestly, you can't ask for much more than that.

We talk a lot about love in our society. And for good reason—it's a many-splendored thing and makes the world go 'round, etc., etc. But it's not all you need—at least not when it comes to long-term commitment.

Scientists who track how we experience romance have found that relationships evolve in predictable ways over time. When we first fall in love, our brains are flooded with a feel-good chemical called dopamine. Suddenly the world looks shiny and new. You hardly need to eat or sleep because you have found perfection incarnate and by some miracle the Most Wonderful Person on Earth actually seems to like you back! You wake up giddy, relive last night's kiss a thousand times in your mind, and count the minutes until you'll be together again.

So that's fun! And it should last you a good month or two. But as the dopamine recedes—and thank God it does or you'd just loll about googly-eyed for the rest of your life—oxytocin levels rise, cementing your bond with a more steady, calming kind of attachment (assuming you can still stand the sight of your lover after the infatuation wears off). This is where the part about actually liking someone comes in. Because in the context of a lifetime, lust is quite brief. I sat down with a couple named Steve and Lisa shortly after their tenth anniversary. They found each other through a personals ad: a real one, in the paper. (I did not ask if they were also still using a rotary telephone, but I'm pretty sure I saw a spiral cord draped on the counter in the kitchen.)

"Yang seeks yin," Steve wrote. "Smart, fun, handsome, 34-year-old SWPM seeks mysterious connection."

Lisa's friends told her not to respond, saying, "He seems weird."

"Yeah, but I'm weird," countered Lisa, before leaving a message in Steve's assigned voice-mail box.

She was the single mother of a young son, and was determined not to compromise herself for anyone. "I was going to be who I am and have my interests and do my thing and if the person I was dating didn't like that, then it wasn't the person for me," she said.

The two met up for a walk that turned into a twelve-hour date. They married the following year. Before long, they'd had two daughters and become a family of five.

We talked about the early years, when they struggled with conflict and crazy schedules and evolving family dynamics. The romance seemed to come and go in waves, but the underlying constant was friendship. When the two first met and even when they said "I do," Lisa didn't realize how much it meant that they really liked each other. They shared a sense of humor and respected one another's idiosyncrasies and intellects. That has made the mundane—even the drudgery—infinitely more bearable.

"When I've felt most close to him is when we have a sick kid and we're up at two in the morning and I'm holding hair back and he's getting a cold compress. We're a team and a unit," she told me. "And we're in it together." Lisa teared up reflecting on how grateful she was to be "married to my best friend."

Someone once told me that marriage is mostly about sitting on the couch with the same person decade after decade. So maybe the question is not: "Who do you want to go to bed with?" But instead: "Who do you want to sit next to?" Hopefully it's someone who will share the remote.

Don't Move In Just to
Save on Rent

Here's a statistic that scared me: Couples who move in together before getting engaged wind up less satisfied in their marriages and more likely to contemplate divorce.

Aaron and I had been dating for about a year when, on a trip to see family, I raised the always entertaining "Where is this going?" question. (Car rides are great for these kind of talks because you have a captive audience—at least until one of you decides to cut your losses and roll out onto the highway.) We started talking about getting a place together. For him it was an important step—he couldn't see getting married until it was clear we could live under the same roof without wanting to kill each other. I had reservations. I wanted to live with him, but I didn't want to feel like the relationship was on trial. And those statistics made me even more nervous, although at first glance, they don't make sense. Wouldn't you think that couples who'd lived together before tying the knot would have the kinks worked out of their relationship and know exactly what they're getting into?

According to the social scientists who've studied this stuff, the answer is: sort of. I spent nearly two hours on the phone with Scott Stanley, a psychology professor at the University of Denver who has researched the effects of cohabitation rates for more than fifteen years. Stanley is kind and smart and earnest, someone you can imagine leading a Cub Scout troop. And if you were thinking about moving in with your boyfriend or girlfriend, Professor Stanley would suggest you reconsider.

The problem, he explained to me, isn't that cohabitation causes people to be less happy in their marriages. It's that cohabitation can lead to marriage for some couples who might otherwise go their separate ways. He calls it "sliding versus deciding."

A couple might decide to move in together without much thought toward the future. They know that they spend a lot of time at each other's places already, and they also know that renting one apartment is cheaper than renting two. So they take the plunge. Months tick by and they start to mingle finances, maybe get a dog or dining room set, eventually buy a house. After a while someone's nosy aunt begins asking questions about when they'll get married. They ignore the pressure at first, but the drumbeat gets louder and louder: *Marriage! Marriage! Marriage!* It becomes a fait accompli.

Even if there are problems in the relationship, it starts to seem like the couple owes it to each other—and to their home viewing audience—to get hitched. And so they do. They slide right into it. Then a few years later one of them admits to being miserable, and tells her friends she knew all along that it wasn't quite right.

This sounds dangerously familiar, right? But cohabitation isn't going anywhere. A study by the Centers for Disease Control and Prevention found that by 2010, 48 percent of women between fifteen and forty-four had lived with a partner they weren't married to. (This also explains why divorce lawyers have seen an increase in litigation between couples who've never tied the knot.)

By the time Aaron and I were discussing moving in together, I had interviewed some very smart couples who said cohabitating was the best thing they ever did. It brought them closer together, turned them into a family, and gave them the opportunity to work on problem areas. I'd also interviewed some very smart couples who decided to hold off until they were married, reasoning that they wanted their vows to mark the start of a sacred commitment and a new, unified life.

I could see the merit in both philosophies. And after talking to Stanley I was a little less worried about choosing one or the other. I realized that the important thing was that Aaron and I were on the same page about what we were doing and where we were headed. It was all about making a conscious decision— and doing it for the sake of commitment, not convenience. Because as Stanley told me: "Commitment means making a choice to give up other choices."

So eighteen months into our relationship, when we were both sure that this thing was headed toward marriage, we moved in together. And despite considerable growing pains— "Is *that* how you wash dishes?" "Obviously my couch is better than your couch"—we still liked each other enough to get engaged six months later.

In the end, I came to the conclusion that living in sin isn't so bad . . . as long as it's about love and not just cheaper rent.

Clash of Civilizations

"It shouldn't be called the 'Honeymoon Period.' It should be called the 'Clash of Civilizations.'" That's what one marriage educator told me about the first few years a couple lives together, which used to start after the wedding, but now often precedes it.

Her point was that we set ourselves up for disappointment. We think moving in together will be all happy times and great sex and picking out china that we'll use for elaborate candlelit dinners on the back patio. Instead, it often includes screaming matches over whose art gets hung where, why you should do the damn dishes since I cooked this meal, and *Can you just go someplace else for a while? I can't think with you breathing over there.*

I found the "Clash of Civilizations" theory to be a great relief. It took the pressure off, and it made sense. For the entirety of my existence, I had done things one way and they had worked perfectly for me. Aaron had done things another way and could not see that my way was vastly superior. It takes time to bring your partner into the light—or, you know, compromise.

When Aimee lived alone, she had decorated her apartment in shades of pink and purple, with soft pillows and frilly accent pieces everywhere. She's a civil rights lawyer and a self-described "girly-girl" who loves high heels, fashion, and makeup. Naturally, she fell in love with a hyperanalytical "manly man" who painted his walls dark red and hung knives and swords in the living room.

"Combining these two aspects of our personalities was interesting," she told me.

I appreciated Aimee's candor. And of course, the aesthetic stuff was superficial. Everything else—how to handle money, work through big decisions, and deal with the rhythms of someone else's life—proved even more difficult. Living together was, she said, "a big adjustment." But eventually it got easier, "after we hammered out all the initial bumps in the road."

Neither of us is a neatnik, but when Aaron and I first moved in together we were appalled by the other's mess. He had boxes full of immaculately filed paperwork, but it didn't bother him to sit in front of a coffee table littered with empty glasses and takeout containers. I, on the other hand, hated the sight of a cluttered surface—which is why I strategically dumped all my junk into whatever drawer or cupboard happened to be available.

This kind of thing can still be an issue, but at least now we know what to expect from each other. I anticipate his complaints about my overstuffed drawers; he expects me to glare wrathfully at his left-behind garbage. Knowing it was normal to feel as though we were in a state of civilization-clashing— rather than pure domestic bliss—made those first months of cohabitation a little easier. We were able to laugh at ourselves and recognize the rite of passage for what it was.

It can be hard, coexisting with another person day in, day out. You have to put up with their smells and bathroom habits and terrible taste in television and that incessant breathing at all hours. And you have to reconcile your whole manner of living with their whole manner of living, despite the fact that their manner of living is obviously absurd.

But you do it because you love them. And because the process also brings sweetness and comfort as you set up house and develop the rituals that will carry you through life. One woman I know described living together as a "permanent sleepover with my best friend."

In the end, putting that framed Pearl Jam poster into storage seems like a small price to pay for life with someone you adore, who makes you a better person and who—perhaps— improves your taste in art.

Fight the Good Fight

Although I'm always unnerved by couples who squabble throughout my interviews, there's another group who worries me just as much: couples who say they've never had a fight.

Really? Because you're simply so simpatico on every conceivable issue that a serious difference of opinion has never crept up? Neither of you has ever unintentionally hurt the other, making some innocent mistake that you never imagined would cause the pain that it did? Or had a bad day and taken it out on the other with a quick word?

Maybe when issues come up, couples like this always have the grace, patience, and emotional intelligence to resolve the problem without even the slightest bump in blood pressure. More likely, however, one or both of them are swallowing their frustration in the name of keeping the peace. Which can last only so long.

I'm well versed in this strategy of conflict management

(read: avoidance) because it was my singular MO before I fell in love with a man for whom no point of contention should go undiscussed and lingering resentments cannot be tolerated. It's exhausting. And, I hate to admit, probably a godsend.

Throughout the second half of the twentieth century, much of the psychological research on relationships focused on the way couples deal with disagreements. It was presumed that this was the make-or-break factor in marriage. Today most psychologists think other elements, including positive interactions and commitment levels, carry equal weight, but there's no question that conflict management skills are crucial to the health of any long-term relationship.

John Gottman is a Seattle psychologist who with Nan Silver wrote the bestselling advice book *The Seven Principles for Making Marriage Work.* He famously claims to be able to predict with 91 percent accuracy whether or not a couple will get divorced, just by watching them interact for five minutes. But they're not just interacting: They're fighting. When couples come to his "Love Lab," they're asked to discuss a tough issue. Gottman says the way each pair tackles conflict tells him everything he needs to know.

"Most marital arguments cannot be resolved," Gottman writes. "Couples spend year after year trying to change each other's minds—but it can't be done." The difference between happy couples and those headed for divorce, according to Gottman, is the way they grapple with their perennial differences.

He fears for a couple's fate when it's apparent that their marriage has become home to what he calls the "Four Horsemen of the Apocalypse": criticism, contempt, defensiveness, and stonewalling. All of these offending behaviors make an appearance in even the most loving relationships, according to Gottman, but couples mired in them are on shaky ground. The good news, however, is that relationships aren't in a fixed state. Couples can learn to alter their argument styles to create more effective patterns of dealing with conflict.

Take Jeremy and Domonique, who met while serving in the National Guard. They liked the same comic books and video games, and she liked him. At first the affection was painfully one-sided. But when he moved to her town, they started going to concerts and movies together and, as months passed, he was drawn in by her loving spirit. Jeremy was the one who finally suggested they make things official.

The pair started spending almost every night together and got along beautifully—except when they didn't. She was inclined to talk about issues that bothered her as soon as they arose. He kept things to himself, until he couldn't stand it anymore. "I'll yell and scream, just really out of anger," Jeremy told me. "Then after, I cool off. That's when the rational side kicks in. Like, 'You just made a jerk out of yourself.'"

Though he was always apologetic, Jeremy's blowups got to be too much for Domonique. She knew he'd been through bad breakups in the past and suspected that when an issue developed, he considered it the beginning of the end.

"I had to be like, 'It's okay for you to be upset. It's okay for you not to agree with me. The ceiling's not gonna fall. The world's not coming to an end. It's actually sometimes a good thing,'" she recalled.

When it became clear to Jeremy that Domonique wasn't going anywhere, that she could deal with the tough moments and loved him even when they didn't see eye to eye, the walls he'd put up started to crumble. "Then he actually learned to sit down and say, 'Okay, look I'm upset, but we'll talk about it,'" recalled Domonique. "I was like, 'Oh! It's like I'm winning the lottery!' And once we got the communication thing down, the relationship snowballed. We can talk about anything."

Soon the two were engaged. At their wedding Domonique arranged for a troupe of *Star Wars* reenactors to surprise Jeremy with a live skit. Then he took the microphone and serenaded her with their favorite song.

Neither one of them expected that they'd never run into trouble again; his tendency to yell hadn't vanished completely. But at least they'd identified the problem, understood each other's perspective, and thought about how to deal with it. Gottman would be proud.

One marriage educator I interviewed said that as a society, we need to change the way we view conflict in relationships. We need to think of it as being like the sound a train makes when it's running at full speed: the inevitable product of two people, two mind-sets, working out issue after issue, day after day. The real problem, she says, is when the noise stops—and the train has ground to a halt.

This is why so many relationship books and training programs focus on learning constructive ways to manage conflict. Soon after we were married, I dragged Aaron to a workshop that taught a listening technique designed to make sure that each person is allowed to fully express themselves before their partner responds. We use it to work through particularly troubling issues, since it inevitably slows the conversation down and allows us to see things from the other's point of view.

The goal is not to put an end to conflict, as if that were even possible. The idea is to embrace it as a natural part of all unions and to use it as a means of driving the relationship forward—not derailing it at every turn.

Just Like Your Mama

"You put your broom where your mother put her broom."

I once wrote a magazine story about seven women—a grand-mother, her five daughters, and her eldest granddaughter—who all wore the same wedding dress. It had been taken in and let out, stained and cleaned and tenderly passed from woman to woman.

I learned a great deal from this family of smart, strong, stubborn women. I learned about the importance of tradi-tion, the comfort and constraints of family, and our ability to love one another through the best and worst of life . . . but mostly I learned that you put your broom where your mother put her broom.

Lambie, the eldest of the five sisters who all had animal nicknames (Bunny, Kitten, Robin, and Dove), was speaking literally when she said this, but she might as well have been explaining the secret truth of all human behavior. Lambie kept her broom in the pantry—"where it belongs." When she was newly married, a sister-in-law visited and was appalled to find that the broom wasn't next to the refrigerator—"where it belongs."

"Whether they tell you or not, you know what people expect of marriage?" Lambie mused. "They expect what they saw in their own household."

If your mom always put onions in her potato salad, chances are good that you put onions in yours. If your husband's father refused to leave for a road trip without checking the oil in the engine, you might as well pop the hood for your spouse before loading up the car.

It's almost unbelievable how much childhood imprints itself on each of us—whether we want it to or not.

Lambie and her sisters shared an industriousness that was a near-perfect reflection of what they saw from their mother, who'd raised seven children and helped her husband build a booming business from scratch.

Lambie deeply admired her mother's incredible work ethic and devotion to her children; she also resented the times when that devotion felt controlling. And once she had kids of her own, she couldn't help but want to hold sway over certain aspects of their lives, even when it caused friction between them.

I don't believe that we all turn into our parents—that seems too simplistic—but we certainly carry them with us, and shouldn't be surprised if we occasionally channel them, in ways both good and bad. And it seems like a pretty crucial premise to bear in mind when trying to understand—and co-exist with—our partners. Is she tight with money? Instead of judging her for only leaving the waiter a 10 percent tip, it might be worth talking about her parents' attitudes toward finances. Perhaps cash was sometimes scarce, so she'd been taught to save at every turn. You don't have to be okay with leaving bad tips, but at least you'll get where she's coming from.

The same applies to just about everything: cleanliness, exercise habits, comfort with physical affection, ideas about gender roles, and toilet paper preference. I, for example, buy whatever brand is on sale. If that happens to be "SandPaper Ultra Thin," so be it. Aaron, on the other hand, only likes the fluffy two-ply with the giggly cartoon mascot. Peace talks are ongoing.

Psychologists have written about how important it is for couples to allow themselves to be influenced by each other, both in thought and behavior. That happens naturally whenever any two people spend a great deal of time together. You begin to use the same phrases and share similar worldviews. But it will take years to match the influence held by one's family. This can be frustrating at the outset, but it's also an opportunity. You both get to see another way of doing things and can then decide together what really works best for the two of you. Do you even *like* onions in your potato salad?

When I sat down with Lambie's sister, Bunny, she told me that one of the secrets of her more than twenty-year marriage was that she and her husband consciously adopted the best of each of their upbringings for their life together. They keep regular date nights, like his parents always did, but are tremendously focused on their children, just as her parents were. "It's the balance," she told me. "We really are a blend." The trick is being open to the possibility that your partner's family traditions could have some advantages—at least occasionally.

I didn't ask Bunny where she kept her broom, but I'd bet it's in the pantry. Exactly where it belongs.

It Takes a Village

The main thing I remember about Tej and Kivneet's wedding is that I did not die. The Sikh ceremony started early on a Friday morning. In India, grooms often make their entrance saddled on an elephant. But seeing as elephants aren't so easy to come by in the United States, Indian American grooms usually opt for a horse (or sometimes even a Harley-Davidson).

Tej was preparing to mount the white stallion, who'd been decked out in a jeweled, red velvet robe for the occasion, when two drummers began pounding a loud, rhythmic beat. I stood among the closely gathered guests, trying—and failing—to be inconspicuous. I was in my usual black dress, while every other woman wore a gorgeous, brightly colored sari. Then, before Tej had even left the ground, the horse got spooked, bucked, and charged into the crowd.

Certain he was coming straight toward me, I took off, knocking down only a few old men and small children blocking my path. Turns out four-inch heels are not the ideal footwear choice for outrunning a stampede. Within a few steps I'd fallen, blood gushing from my knee.

Everyone thinks foreign war correspondents have the most dangerous job in journalism; no one ever considers the hardships of a wedding reporter.

Inconspicuous no more, I quivered as people started asking if they should call an ambulance. "No, no," I bravely responded. But my grave injury did require a Band-Aid. And I still have a small scar. I'm sure the *Post* is grateful I didn't file for worker's compensation.

The next thing I remember about Tej and Kivneet's wedding, though, is that I have never felt so engulfed in love. Not just in the wake of my little accident, but for the rest of the ceremony and the next day, when five hundred friends and relatives packed into a hotel ballroom, all of them—from the youngest men to the oldest aunties—dancing wildly in celebration of the couple.

Before the wedding, Kivneet knew she would be surrounded by this kind of warmth, even if she didn't know much else. She had, after all, met Tej only three times before she agreed to move across the world to marry him.

They were first introduced when a friend who grew up with Tej met Kivneet in India and gave them each other's email addresses. Tej's older brother encouraged him to send a note. Soon they were trading daily messages. When Kivneet's long-planned trip to the United States brought her to Washington, D.C., the pair met at the birthplace of many American romances—a Starbucks. They were instantly at ease with each other and spent the next day wandering through a park.

"It's funny because we're from opposite sides of the world, yet we were still able to meet halfway and talk about so many things," Tej recalled.

At the end of her eighteen-day trip, Kivneet, a doe-eyed beauty with long dark hair, arranged to return to D.C. to have dinner with Tej's family, a gathering that normally wouldn't happen unless a wedding was in the works.

Though they both knew it was a leap of faith, Tej soon proposed and Kivneet accepted. Extremely close to her family and friends, Kivneet was deeply nervous about leaving India, but she wasn't counting solely on Tej to welcome her. Once she arrived, she'd be living with Tej's parents, brother, and sister-in-law. Any children they had would be raised among cousins and grandparents. The minute her plane landed she would feel the embrace of this family and community.

Tej might be the focal point of Kivneet's new life, but he would not be the whole of it. And it was this fact that made her most confident about the future of her marriage. Which, incidentally, has turned out to be a very happy one.

I am not suggesting that we all move to a commune or build a new wing for the in-laws. But Kivneet's story is an interesting antidote to a common issue in modern American relationships: We expect our spouse to be our everything.

Whoever we marry should be our best friend and our soul mate, our closest confidant, intellectual equal, traveling companion, co-parent, sole support system, tennis partner, and sous chef. In the off-hours, they're welcome to have their own life and bring home a six-figure salary.

It's possible that's a *bit* too much weight to place on one person's shoulders.

And it's only in recent generations that we would even consider it. Many of our grandparents and great-grandparents spent their whole lives in one place, surrounded by siblings, cousins, aunts, and uncles who lived next door or up the block. Lots of people played a hand in child rearing and there were plenty of folks to help out whenever someone got sick. If you were sad or scared or frustrated there was a small army of supporters ready to pass you a tissue.

Now many of us live far from our families and even for those in the same town, the nuclear unit is tighter and more isolating than it once was. Some sociologists have pointed to this trend as a factor in our national divorce rate—which is particularly high in states with transient populations.

A lot has been written about the positive health benefits of marriage. Married people—especially married men—live longer, more satisfying lives than their single counterparts. But community is an important factor, too. A study of middle-aged men and women in the United Kingdom found that having a wide circle of friends and associates was key to psychological well-being. Of course it is. More friends means more fun outings, more emotional support, and more pinch-hit babysitters.

In the middle of Tej and Kivneet's wedding reception, Tej's dad requested a microphone to toast his new daughter-in-law. "I'm going to expect a lot from you," he told her. "Lots and lots of love." Kivneet smiled and nodded, assured that everything she gave would be returned in spades.

We'd all be wise to cultivate that same kind of support system. If family is far away, your community might consist of close friends, neighbors, co-workers, or even professional counselors: Anyone you can rely on, so that your partner doesn't crumble under the pressure of your unending needs.

Because sometimes, when you're running from a horse, the love of your life can't be by your side to watch you bite the dust. But, if you're lucky, you'll be surrounded by a crowd of kindly allies who will get you patched up just the same.

How Will I Know?

"You'll just know." Have three more infuriating words ever been thrown together?

"Oh, you'll just know," the newly smug bride-to-be announces to her single girlfriends over brunch. "You'll just know when it's right."

How will you know? I suppose in the same way you'll *just know* when it's time to toss a mimosa in her face.

I routinely tried to press people on this point during interviews. "How did you know she was the one?" "How did you know you wanted to marry him?"

"I just knew."

"Yes, but *how* did you know?"

"I don't know. I just knew."

So I'd ask it another way. "What was it that made you sure?" "What did you feel this time that was different from past relationships?"

Often I'd get more of the same. My subjects just knew it in their bones or in their soul or in the deepest recesses of their very being. I don't mean to be dismissive of this description—I think it's both apt and accurate for the people who experience it—it's just also frustratingly inexact.

There is no decision in life more consequential than whom to marry. And the pressure to choose correctly can be paralyzing—or worse, blinding. You've been together for years, like each other well enough, and don't fight too much: *Is this it?* Or you met three months ago and now can't seem to breathe without them: *Maybe this is it?*

Hopefully, *you'll just know,* but in the meantime, it might help to examine some of the smoke signals that led others to believe they'd found the real thing.

Sometimes when I try to get people to explain the inexplicable—and I do realize that's what I'm asking of them—they tell me a story. Usually these stories do a better job than a straightforward description in pointing to how they experience their partner's love as something nourishing and familiar. Something that feels like home.

Dana, an environmental activist in her late thirties, was in the midst of a divorce when she first spotted Dennis and his dog around the neighborhood. Conversations at the dog park led to dinner at the restaurant where Dennis worked as a chef. Soon there were beers on her front porch and an emerging intimacy. With Dennis, Dana was softer, more affectionate, and more emotionally naked than she'd been with anyone else. But she was scared of being hurt again, so she threw up roadblocks at every turn.

Finally her resistance got to be too much. Dennis told her he couldn't handle it anymore. "It was just really hard," she told me. "Because I kinda knew I did that to myself—or to us."

But a few weeks after their breakup she came home to find a package waiting. Inside was a bat box: a birdhouse-like structure meant for bats. Anyone else might have been freaked-out, but to Dana it was the most meaningful gift she'd ever received. She loved bats, as Dennis knew, and had once mentioned wanting a habitat like this for them. Tears streamed down her face as she realized how thoroughly Dennis understood her. He listened, got who she really was, and loved her without reservation. "He showed me so much caring and loving, it kind of broke me down," she said. And a year later, she was the one to propose.

Jennifer, a pretty blonde who'd once been an NBA cheerleader, had always prided herself on her toughness and independence. She'd been raised by a single mom, put herself through college, established a thriving career in policy, and bought her own condo in Washington, D.C. And as one romance after another failed, she decided she'd rather be alone than go through the wringer one more time.

So when Jim, an exuberant Ivy League graduate who had

served in the military, studied Buddhism, and set up a non-profit in Africa, showed up at a dinner party Jennifer was throwing, she was a little skeptical. He asked to take her out flying in an airplane; she agreed to dinner instead. But his optimism offset her apprehension. And he just kept showing up—planning dates, making her laugh, listening as she spoke.

Before long, she began to feel something she hadn't felt before: safe. "My whole life I feel like I've just been this little fighter. I'm like, 'Fight, fight, fight, fight. Go, go, go, go.' And with him I could be sweet and sincere in a way that I didn't feel made me vulnerable," she said.

And once he found the real Jennifer, Jim didn't want to let go. "When I was in relationships in the past, they'd always create a little panic in me," he said. "Whether there was a need from the other partner that I couldn't fulfill or just a real nervousness about what the future would look like. Jen was the first person in my entire life where none of that panic was there."

I've often told people about the *Post*'s advice columnist Carolyn Hax's response to a reader who wondered how she would know if she had found "the One," five years into a relationship. Carolyn posited these questions, among others: "Do you refresh, not exhaust, each other?" "Would you be with this person even if you couldn't marry or have kids—i.e., if there were no societal ticket to punch?" "Okay, s/he's wonderful. But is s/he wonderful for you?"

I picked up one of the sagest pieces of wisdom of my life

while eavesdropping on a conversation between a yoga instructor and her friend. They were discussing a career decision the woman had to make. "Your body always knows what's right," the yogi said. "You can lie to yourself mentally, but not physically." If I had heard that sooner, it might have saved me a lot of time. I remember so distinctly feeling jittery around some boyfriends and clenched around others—and these were people I liked! But there was always a moment of relief, of being able to exhale, whenever they left the room.

So to Carolyn's list of questions, I would add a couple of others: Do you actually want to be around this person? Especially when it's just the two of you and there's nothing particularly fun going on and there's no booze involved?

Have you laughed significantly more than you've cried since they came into your life? All relationships generate some drama, but if it's brought you more angst than joy—or more tears than you'd normally have on your own—then that's something to pay attention to.

Did I "just know" with Aaron? I suppose so. Mostly what I knew was that I was always looking forward to the next thing. The next date, and then the next month and year and stage of life. I knew I wanted there to be a "next" and felt pretty confident that he did, too. But I don't think that all these couples who walk around proudly "knowing" never have any doubts. The honest ones will tell you they do. Sometimes things get extraordinarily tough and it seems like too much and they wonder if life would be easier with somebody else, or alone.

But the doubts are routinely overridden by the solace they've found in their partner. Eventually things stop seeming so bad. Maybe there's a hug or a sigh or a begrudging laugh. They settle back into the warm, soft spot next to the one they love, knowing they're already home.

BREAKUPS

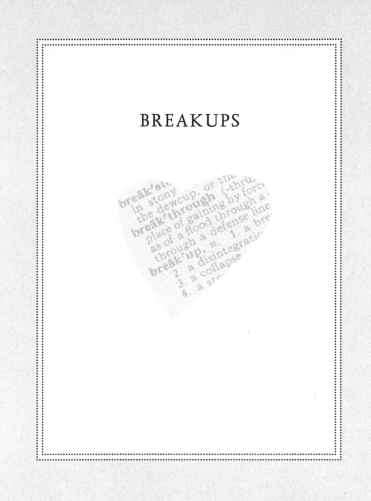

break'st...
in stony
the dewcup, or the...
break'through (-thru,...
place of gaining by forc...
as of a flood through a...
through a defense line...
break'up, n. 1. a bre...
  2. a disintegrati...
  3. a collapse...
  4. a sp...

With my first serious boyfriend, I was the dumper. With the second I was dumped. (Twice, actually—it's a long story.) And with my third, in the relationship that ended just as I started the weddings beat, it was mutual.

For the record, each breakup was horrible.

Maybe it's a tiny bit better when you're the dumper and you know what's coming and have some sense of control. But then you also have to deal with the anxiety leading up to the split and the tidal wave of guilt that comes after. And you still have all the garden-variety sadness besides.

In the movie version of my life, I would have spent my youth dating assholes before finally wising up and falling for a decent human being. But the truth is I mostly dated nice men who treated me well. (Or at least as well as could be expected from guys in their late teens and twenties.) The fact that they were good people didn't make things easier. In some ways, the breaks could've been cleaner had they been jerks. As it was, we just had to come to the sad, slow conclusion that this wasn't it. Whatever it is we're all looking for, we didn't find it with each other.

Like I said: always horrible.

But if you believe in some basic benevolence of the universe, as I tend to, you can tell yourself that it was never all for naught. That the relationships that didn't work out still served a purpose, teaching you about yourself and your needs, preparing you to be a better partner down the road.

And the same goes for breakups. Hopefully, on a glass-half-full kind of day—probably months after one or the other of you said, "We need to talk . . ."—you'll be able to look back and recognize all the ways you're stronger and more resilient for having gone through the split, as awful as it was.

Or maybe you'll just look back and think, "Ugh."

But, hey—you're looking back! That means you survived! And who knows what beautiful, future ex could be right around the corner . . .

When to Walk

If it's not right, do *not* go through with the wedding.

If you know in your heart of hearts that something is missing, or slightly off, or that you got engaged mostly out of a sense of obligation—to your fiancé, to your family or theirs, or to society in general—please call it off.

I realize that it will be the hardest thing you've ever had to do. And that it gets harder with each passing day as vendors are paid, toasts are offered, gifts are unwrapped, and flights are booked.

Still. Call it off. Whatever agony you endure or havoc you wreak, it will be minuscule in comparison to the turmoil of a bad marriage or the torment of divorce. Do everything possible to block out the insanity of wedding planning and the noise of other people's voices, so that you can really listen to yourself. What is your heart telling you?

Everyone has occasional doubts. But if yours gnaw at you,

if you wake up with a pit in your stomach and a growing feeling of dread as the wedding approaches, *call it off.*

Psychology researchers at the University of California, Los Angeles, found that women who had serious doubts before their weddings were two and a half times more likely to divorce within four years than women without such misgivings. Another study, in Canada, found that couples who were confident going into marriage were more satisfied with their relationships as the years went on. Meaning, if it's not right *now*, it will only be worse once you tie the knot.

I know that the prospect seems unfathomable. That the shame and guilt will be colossal. That you worry about breaking your best friend's heart—just because you're not sure you should be marrying them doesn't mean you don't love them—and about letting everyone down, and about figuring out what life will look like if you're not together.

But you give everyone too much credit. Let me assure you, they are far too busy worrying about themselves and their own problems to spend an awful lot of time on yours. Broken engagements make great gossip for a week or so, and then everyone moves on. You know who will have a harder time with the consequences of a regretted marriage? Your future children, as they endure the divorce of their parents. If you can't figure out what to do, consider what's best for them.

My brother broke off an engagement six months before the wedding. A friend called hers off while she stood in her bridal suite, hours away from the ceremony. I've never admired their strength more. They did the right, not the easy, thing. And as excruciatingly sad as each situation was, at least four lives are better off today because of their bravery.

Gifts can be returned. Flights can be canceled. You'll be surprised—people understand. And if you're out some money on deposits, so be it.

It doesn't matter how long you've been together, how old you are, or whether you're standing outside the church waiting for the doors to open—if you know you shouldn't go through with it, don't.

For your sake, and for theirs.

Top Ten Reasons to Call It Off

When I'm at a party and people learn what I do for a living, they routinely ask three questions:

1. *"Where do you find couples to write about?"* Some of them submit a questionnaire to the *Post*, but more often I hear about them from deejays, wedding planners, florists, cake makers, and officiants who know what I'm looking for in a story.

2. *"What* are *you looking for in a story?"* Well . . . a story. As lovely as they are, the couples I *can't* write about are the ones who met as college sophomores, fell in love, have been together continuously for four years, are now getting married at age twenty-six and have never encountered any real obstacles. (Unless it's January and I'm desperate to fill the page, in which case I'll take what I can get.)

3. *"Do you ever interview a couple who you think won't make it?"*
God, yes. It's the worst. I often meet with couples the week before their weddings and sometimes by the end of the interview I want to shut off my tape recorder and say, "Listen, guys. It's Wednesday. Your wedding is not until Saturday. You don't have to do this. We can call this off; I'll start notifying the guests." I don't, of course. I just hope they come to their senses and cancel the wedding themselves. (One groom actually did, but not before 160 guests boarded planes to the Dominican Republic for the destination wedding. I promise, it was still for the best.)

With that in mind, here are some signs that you should maybe rethink that long walk down the aisle. All are based on actual interviews:

1. You spend the entire ninety-minute conversation about why you love each other bickering, while sitting on opposite couches with your arms crossed.

2. All of your closest friends are boycotting the wedding because they loathe your fiancé and abhor the way he or she treats you. "They're just jealous," you insist. No. They're not.

3. All of your major relationship milestones—first date, first "I love you's" and engagement—occurred when you've been drunk, high, or otherwise incapacitated.

4. All of your major relationship milestones occurred within a two-week period.

5. When asked to describe your future spouse, the only words you can come up with are "highly annoying."

6. If what you love most about your future spouse is any of the following: a) "She's hot"; b) "He's rich"; c) [Long silence while you stare at the floor, hold your cheek in your hand, and sigh, "This is hard."]

7. Discussing your personal love story is so taxing and/or boring that you literally fall asleep in the middle of an interview.

8. You either proposed or accepted a proposal under an ultimatum (for example, "If I don't see a ring by midnight on December thirty-first, we're through.").

9. Any of the following rank as your *sole* motivation for getting married: health-care benefits, tax breaks, alimony potential, getting your parents off your back already.

10. Your avatars got married in Second Life and that worked out, so you figure this will, too. It happened, I swear.

Beware the Sunk Cost

There is a theory in economics known as the "sunk cost effect." I know almost nothing about economics, but my very smart friend Neil Irwin writes about it for a living and agreed to explain the concept to us.

Take it away, Neil:

"The idea of sunk cost is that in making a decision, you should only take into account future costs and benefits. The past doesn't matter. The sunk cost fallacy is the mistake people make when they don't take this into account. For example, suppose you buy tickets to a basketball game. The night of the game comes around, and you are feeling sick, and the weather is bad, and you would really rather just stay at home and watch the game on television. A lot of people would let the fact that they had already paid for tickets lead them to trudge to the game even though they really don't want to. But it should be irrelevant! You're not getting that money back either way, so the wise thing to do is to go to the game only if the enjoyment of being there will be worth the cost of trudging to the arena in the rain despite being sick."

You can imagine why the sunk cost bias is so dangerous when it comes to relationships.

Let's say you have been with Person X for three, four, or five years. You have built up a trove of memories with them— mountains climbed, vacations taken, arguments fought and resolved. You've met their parents and introduced them to yours. You jointly bought a couch and impulsively adopted a rescue dog from the pound. Together, you named him Oscar.

Your whole current existence is built around this person. And you've put so much into this relationship that it seems like you owe it to him or her—to both of you, really—to keep it going.

Don't do it. The fact that you've invested however many years of your life in this person is not a reason to invest however many more. If you are thinking about the time you've lost, the years that would be "wasted" if you were to end the relationship today, you are falling prey to sunk cost bias.

The only question you need to concern yourself with is this: What do you want for the rest of your life? If many continued years of what you have with this person sounds appealing, then great. Go look at diamonds! But if the thought of a half century more of the same makes you slightly queasy, then it's probably time to take a hard look at why you're still here.

Guilt is not an economic term. It's also not a reason to stay together. Yes, you are a good person and you want to do the right thing and you don't want to break anybody's heart, or anybody's grandmother's heart. But Grandma will survive (at least for a while). And if guilt is your main motivation in keeping this relationship going, please know that you are not doing anyone a favor. It may seem like you're acting out of kindness now—averting tears and heartache—but you're just setting you both up for a much more severe bout of grief in the future. A relationship that hinges on a sense of obligation will not get better. It will get worse.

An ex-boyfriend once left me with what I still believe is among the greatest breakup lines of all time. He said, "When I met you I knew you were gonna make some guy really happy and I wanted that guy to be me. But when I'm really honest with myself, I know that it's not." Now, he receives an automatic four-point deduction on the breakup grading scale because this line was delivered over the phone. While I sat in my car in a parking garage. On a Friday night. On our one-year anniversary. In more ways than one, he did a good job of telling me I deserved better.

The person you love—but maybe are not in love with— also deserves better. But they won't have the chance to find it until you set them free.

And neither will you.

The Aftermath

As a society, we underestimate the devastation that breakups wreak. In many ways it is like experiencing a death, except that you don't get any condolence notes or bereavement days. No one sends out a sympathetic announcement to your co-workers. There is no established ritual whereby your friends and family come together to help you cope with your grief. Most of the time, no one even bothers to drop off a casserole.

But still, you sit alone, with your arms wrapped around your knees, certain you will never be loved again.

Perhaps the worst part is that the person you've come to rely on for support and comfort can't help you. They're back at their place, also curled up in the fetal position. *Except*, says a little voice, *they could help*. They're right over there, but somehow you're expected to have enough self-control not to reach out to them.

And suddenly you have to reimagine everything. Your

whole future—where you'll live, what you'll name your children, whom you'll be buried next to. And, more pressing: what you'll do with yourself tomorrow night. And the night after that. And the night after that.

It's no wonder that researchers have found that our very sense of self is rattled by breakups. Psychologists from Northwestern University conducted three different studies that reached the same conclusion: We're less sure of who we are on our own after losing our "better half." Even if that half isn't actually better, at least for you. And even if logically you know you really will be better off without this relationship. That doesn't make it any easier to give up on the dreams you concocted together. Or to face the terrifying prospect that you might never encounter anything that good again, and that the only way to find out is to try to start dating, which sounds like the most miserable idea ever.

Also, society tells us, you should grapple with everything without missing a beat at work or school. And try not to kill the mood during happy hour with your friends, okay?

It might be a good idea for us to cut one another some slack and offer a little more support. So I propose that we redefine the bachelor/bachelorette party. Instead of occurring pre-wedding, it should happen post-breakup—you know, when you're actually a bachelor or bachelorette. And when you might want to go out and drink too much and flirt with strangers. And when you really need something to look forward to. Obviously this ritual wouldn't take away the pain of a breakup. But it could help remind the newly single of how much they're loved and how much fun life can be.

But even if it doesn't necessarily include a booze-fueled fiesta, we should rethink our societal perspective on breakups. They're not small bumps in the road. They feel like catastrophic, life-altering events and in many ways they are.

Ideally they happen for the right reasons, and ultimately open life up to bigger, better possibilities. But the hope for a silver lining doesn't necessarily dull the ache. And a little understanding of that could go a long way.

Breakups Hurt. Literally.

In one of the greatest Motown hits ever, singer Jimmy Ruffin wondered, "What becomes of the brokenhearted?"

Finally science has provided an answer: They basically become crack addicts. Or, more precisely, crack addicts who can't find their next fix and are stooped over on the sidewalk, trying to crawl out of their own skin.

Think back to your last breakup. Sounds about right, doesn't it?

Renowned psychologist Art Aron saw one student after another at Stony Brook University become unhinged by heartache. And of course, he'd often enough experienced the same feelings himself. So after thirty years of studying romantic relationships, he decided to figure out what exactly happens when we've lost that lovin' feeling.

He teamed up with other researchers and recruited some students who'd been rejected romantically. Aron's subjects admitted they thought obsessively about the object of their affection for more than 85 percent of their waking hours. They also cried incessantly, begged to get back together, called and emailed at all hours, and took to drinking. You know the drill.

I caught up with Professor Aron by phone and he seemed perfectly nice—but he did not let that stand in the way of science. He hooked up his subjects to brain monitors and showed them two pictures: One of someone they knew casually and one of the ex who rejected them. And Aron found that when people looked at their lost love, the areas of the brain that light up are the same as those associated with addiction and cravings.

Meaning, when we go through heartbreak, we experience withdrawal. Which explains the shaking, the nausea, the longing for our ex's particular smell and touch. It also explains why we so often move on to a new relationship immediately: We're looking for our next fix.

It's important to understand what's happening when we face a breakup, so that we can be a little gentler with ourselves and each other. And the findings may suggest, as Aron told me, that we "look at things that have been helpful in getting people over specific addictions to help people deal with these kinds of situations." (Maybe we can set up clinics for the recently dumped. It would probably make for a great singles scene.)

Breakups really are that traumatizing. Another group of researchers found that when someone who was rejected romantically looks at a picture of their ex, the same parts of their brain that register physical pain are activated. And a study out of Johns Hopkins University discovered that it's possible to literally die of a broken heart. Severe emotional traumas flood the body with stress hormones that can stun the heart and cause it to malfunction in a way that mimics a heart attack.

So be nice to your colleague who just got the boot. And be patient with your friend who is *still*, however many months later, obsessing over her horrible ex. If you're the one who's grieving try to be kind to yourself. Know that what you're going through is real and raw and truly excruciating. No one escapes it. We're mortal, so loss is implicit in love.

But drug addicts who go through recovery find that, with time, the gnawing desire for their next hit starts to lose its grip. The same goes for heartache. There will always be pangs of longing, but as the days tick by, you'll grow healthier, more whole, and ready for a new chapter of life to begin.

Moving On

Now that we've learned that breaking up really *is* hard to do, it might be useful to look at some coping mechanisms that researchers have found effective in helping people heal and move on after a split.

Perhaps the main thing to keep in mind is that you can't dodge the pain. You can numb it temporarily with Pinot Gris or Ben & Jerry's, but in the end whatever detours you take to avoid the hurt will only prolong it. So first of all, give yourself the time and latitude to cry, mope, and wallow. Nothing will allow you to sidestep the stages of grief. And remember what you already know about dealing with stress: You've got to eat right, exercise, be kind to yourself, and seek out professional help if the misery starts to feel like more than you can manage.

This untenable ache will ease with time, but the quicker the better, yes? So without further ado, here are some strategies that may speed the process and lessen the pain.

1. Write it out. Psychologists have found journaling to be helpful for people in all kinds of distressing situations. But chronicling your reflections on a breakup can be especially healing, one study found. A group of students who'd recently left relationships were asked to spend fifteen to thirty minutes a day writing at home. A third of the students were instructed to detail the positive aspects of their breakup—how their lives were better off. Another third covered the negative aspects—ways in which their breakups were difficult. The last group wrote about an unrelated, superficial topic. The researchers found that those who spent time reflecting on the ways their lives were improved saw an increase in positive emotions regarding the split. They felt happier, more empowered and more energetic.

2. While you're at it, try to focus on the breakup as an opportunity for growth. Psychologists believe that when people concentrate on the lessons they learned from a relationship and the ways their lives can expand now that it's over—perhaps by freeing them up to pursue new paths—they feel more resolution and closure.

3. Speaking of closure . . . try to get some. Breakups rarely come in one fell swoop. As Jerry explained to Elaine in *Seinfeld*, "Breaking up is like knocking over a Coke machine. You can't do it in one push. You've got to rock it back and forth a few times, and then it goes over."

But if you're really ready to be done, approach the break with purpose: Have a decided, final conversation with your ex or write them a letter expressing your feelings about the relationship. Say whatever it is you need to get off your chest and, if you can, wish them well in their life. Then get back to moving on with your own.

4. Go on the rebound. That doesn't mean marriage—just have some fun. Go on a date. Make out with a stranger in a dark bar. Start surfing online dating profiles to remind yourself how many potential prospects are out there. Psychologists have found that focusing on someone new can help you let go of your ex. In this instance, Mr. or Ms. Right Now is *exactly* right.

5. Fill the void. As humans, we're designed to get deeply attached to other people. It's how we form families and propagate the species. Our romantic partner often becomes what psychologists call our "primary attachment figure," the person we want to talk to about everything that happens to us (good, bad, or utterly mundane). With a breakup, we're cut off from that fundamental source of comfort. Let others—your friends, family, your favorite Internet buddies—pick up the slack. Let them listen to your stories and be your sounding boards and activity partners. That will help you make room for someone new, when he or she comes along, and be open to all the goodness they have to offer.

WEDDINGS

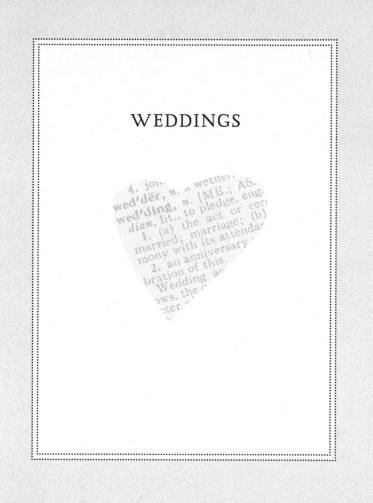

I began my journalism career as a business and technology reporter. My family found this hysterical. They knew that I didn't own a cell phone, couldn't balance a checkbook, and in third grade had to be placed in the remedial math class because my arithmetic skills were found to be on par with those of the average cocker spaniel. (They still are, but now I own a calculator. Take that, math teachers.)

It seemed equally preposterous when, seven years later, I switched from writing about arts and entertainment to the weddings beat. I had never been married, obviously, and while I'd served as a reluctant brides-maid a couple of times, I knew next to nothing about the modern wedding industry. Except that it seemed like a crock of bull.

I kept my cynicism to myself when applying for the gig. As I've said, I wanted the chance to write about people, and I loved the idea of telling one of the most intimate stories of their lives. But the whole big-dress-and-bigger-budget, it's-my-day-so-I'll-ride-around-in-a-vintage-Rolls-

Royce aspect of weddings seemed like a dark tyranny constructed by an army of clipboard-carrying event planners in stilettos.

Once I got the job, I refused to open the wedding magazines that began filling my office mailbox. Scanning the headlines was enough to scare me: "Autumn's Must-Have Centerpiece: The Squash!" "Napkin Holders to Dazzle Every Guest!" "Your Other Major Life Decision: Which Hairpiece Will It Be?"

I had nightmares about drowning in a sinkhole of satin and lace.

Then I started spending my Saturday nights at weddings. From the periphery I watched fathers try to hold themselves together as they walked their daughters down the aisle. I saw little children dance exuberantly when they had the whole floor to themselves. I lost my breath when tough-guy grooms choked up, speaking about the love that had saved them, a love they promised to protect forever.

Every week, something happened. Two people's lives changed indelibly. And, in spite of myself, I started to believe.

At one wedding, a Hindu priest explained that in India, wedding invitations were extended to whole villages; the more people present to witness the nuptials and celebrate the occasion, they believe, the more blessings that are bestowed on the couple. In Judaism, similarly, it's considered a mitzvah (good deed), to generate as much happiness as possible for a bride and groom.

Weddings matter. Not just because they mark a significant turning point in a couple's lives, which they do. Weddings also serve as rare reunions for extended families and long-lost friends. They are a continuation of sacred rites and centuries-old traditions. And, most important, they are an opportunity for joy. We don't have enough of those in this harried, workaholic society—whole days set aside just to eat and drink and dance and be together. This is the real gift of the wedding, and it's given both to the couple and to everyone lucky enough to be present at their union.

So, I was a convert. And that lasted right up until the moment Aaron proposed and we started to plan our own wedding. Then I finally opened those wedding magazines. "Craft Your Wedding into a DIY Dream!" "Picking the Right Ring Bearer and Other Big Day Dilemmas." All of a sudden people started asking about "our colors" and "my theme." Uh, white? Can the theme be marriage?

Though I knew better, I fell into the clutches of the industry and found myself tossing and turning in the middle of the night, stressed out about budgets and guest lists and all the other garden-variety wedding issues. People kept telling me to "enjoy the process." I kept resisting the urge to punch them in the face.

In the end, though, our wedding was magical. The sun shone on that November day and we exchanged vows at twilight in a grove of linden trees. Everything turned out beautifully.

The next morning, in a fog of exhaustion and hangovers, Aaron asked, "Do you think it was worth it?" Tugging at the fake lashes still glued to my eyes, I shrugged. "I guess so."

"Yeah," he responded. "Probably."

But very quickly our "probably" shifted to "definitely." The leftover anxiety receded as we reflected on the way our nieces had twirled in their pretty dresses, how our mothers had beamed and fathers laughed and *siblings danced. That night our cousins took shots together and our friends got drunk. Some of them even made out with each other, which is really the most a bride and groom can ever hope for.*

My cynicism pendulum has swung somewhere back in the middle now. I still believe that weddings matter. And I will happily come to yours, or anyone's, and dance and drink and toast to good health and enduring happiness. I will be so grateful that someone went to the trouble of putting on a wedding—and even more grateful that someone wasn't me.

Most of all, I'll feel honored to once again witness that extraordinary moment when something happens and two lives are changed forever.

We Did It Our Way

Now that I've admitted that I believe in weddings, I have a request: Marry in a way that's meaningful to you. Please?

And by "you," I mean "you, the two people who plan to marry each other." Not "you, the one who happens to have two X chromosomes" or "you, your cavalcade of bossy relatives, your circle of sorority sisters, and the prevailing expectations of your greater metro area."

One of my favorite weddings took place by a riverbank on a freezing January morning, with just the officiant and three guests present. It felt like we were the only people in the world, gathered to watch a secret miracle. Another took place in a courthouse, where a pair of old friends, who'd both become widows in their fifties, married wearing jeans and red Chuck Taylors. Their grown children cheered when they kissed and then everybody went out to lunch. And I'll never forget the couple who were married by a friend in a public park before hosting a Sunday-afternoon pig roast for fifty friends and relatives.

None of these weddings were fancy or particularly expensive. They probably wouldn't make for a great spread in a glossy magazine. But they were perfect—heartfelt and joyful and sincere. There was no question about the couple's intention: It was to marry each other, not just to have a big party or enjoy a day in the spotlight or appease long-suffering parents.

This is not to say that big parties aren't fabulous or that I wouldn't be delighted to sip a few whiskey drinks at yours. But make sure the big party is what *you* really want, and that you have the chance to do it in a way that feels celebratory, sacred, and authentic to you.

Because after the ring comes out of the box, you have approximately five minutes to revel in the romance before people start asking if you have a date and location and a preference on bridesmaids' hairstyles. And then it's a runaway train. Everyone you encounter—coworkers, future in-laws, that neighbor down the hall you've never previously spoken to—will feel at liberty to tell you what you absolutely must do, can't do, and should have done already:

"Start a binder!"

"Put Great-Uncle Freddy on the list. I don't care that you've never met him. He'll be so hurt if he doesn't get invited!"

"Hire three photographers immediately. You need at least that many to capture every moment and the good ones book up twenty-four months in advance!"

My favorite period of wedding planning was the two months before Aaron and I actually got engaged. Without telling anyone else, we booked a place and a date. For eight weeks we got to be excited about the wedding, but we didn't actually have to *do* anything or talk about it with anyone. It was a glorious time. (Although Aaron would note that I was not the one navigating the diamond-buying process or planning a proposal during those months. So at least it was a glorious time for one of us!)

Our "secret engagement" might seem anticlimactic, but as one bride put it, "The proposal can be a surprise, but the intention to marry shouldn't be." And the real benefit of those two months was that it gave us the chance to figure out what really mattered to us, before the masses started weighing in.

A couple of hundred weddings into my career, I can promise you: There is absolutely nothing you *have* to do, and nothing you *can't* do. You don't have to host a next-day brunch, you don't have to serve a plated dinner, you don't have to invite your former best friend from elementary school or hire a band or even have a reception at all. And if it's what you want, you can get married by an ordained stand-up comedian, have your rings delivered by a hawk, or wear a red dress and black lipstick to your wedding on the Day of the Dead. It's your call! (All true stories, by the way.)

Though there will be enormous pressure to please other people, and you may have to make some compromises for the sake of family peace, it has to feel right to you. Otherwise, forget it.

I admired the couple—both of them introverts—who found themselves immediately overwhelmed by the wedding-planning process and decided halfway through that they'd rather elope and host just a small dinner for their immediate families. More than once I've been to big church weddings where guests were invited only to a ceremony and were sent home with a cupcake afterward. And you know what? Everyone seemed touched and honored to be there—not angry that they weren't also served a mediocre chicken dinner.

At the end of the day, those couples were every bit as married as the ones who threw traditional, big, white weddings. There are a million ways to make the occasion magical. You just have to figure out which is really the right one for you.

Planning Hell

Soon after Aaron and I got engaged, my friend Nick congratulated us with the following wish: "Good luck with all that—if you can get through wedding planning, you deserve to be married."

Pretty soon I knew what he meant.

There are people who eat up the rigors of planning. Who relish the logistical challenges and love the orderly look of a color-coded binder, who desperately want the drumbeat of tiny details and long to-do lists to last forever. But I suspect that even they, somewhere along the line, end up at the breaking point, crying into a satin "bride-to-be" sash as they sit in the chaos of one too many do-it-yourself projects gone wrong.

It seems like planning shouldn't be *that* bad. Like there must be a way to avoid the angst and obsession and stamp-licking psychosis. (And there is. Throughout my engagement my father kept spelling out his favorite five-letter word: *e-l-o-p-e*.)

You think, logically, that you're just throwing a party. People have parties all the time without experiencing major trauma. Draw up a guest list, figure out a menu, throw on a nice outfit, and greet your guests with a smile at the door.

But weddings are exponentially, infinitely worse. In every possible way that a situation could be fraught, they are fraught. How many times have you been told not to mix family and money? Or business and pleasure? Or champagne and Valium?

Yet these are the foundations on which a wedding is built.

Weddings have a nifty way of bringing to a boil every simmering area of potential conflict in life. Has your mom always been slightly controlling, though you've managed to keep those forces at bay for most of adulthood? Not anymore! She's going to want to have some say over every last welcome bag. If you and your beloved have even slightly differing money management strategies, duck and cover! Or perhaps your future in-laws hold divergent views on a tiny little topic like, say . . . God.

Do you want to know what wedding planners talk about when they're together? I've listened, and it's not about their most inspired centerpieces or flower arrangements. They talk about the time when the bride's and groom's parents had both divorced and remarried and it was their job to run interference throughout the wedding because none of the four parental units would speak to each other and all of them thought they were picking up too much of the tab.

And those pitfalls—family dynamics, money, religion—are just the old, standard-issue ones. Now we've entered an era when weddings have taken on a towering new sense of consequence. We want them to define who we are and what we believe, while being just as lovely and fun and maybe somehow *a little bit better* than the weddings of all our closest friends.

Oh, and we must pull this off with the "help" of the whole Internet and Pinterest in particular. These resources primarily work to ensure that if you ever make the mistake of feeling like you're generally on top of things or not a thoroughly inadequate human being, you'll be presented with an endless stream of evidence to the contrary. Have you hand-embroidered souvenir handkerchiefs for each guest yet? And where are you on the ship-in-a-bottle escort cards?

So I really only have one piece of advice in dealing with planning: Keep. It. Short.

Aaron and I were engaged for eight months. It was at least two months too many. The longer the engagement, the longer you spend trapped in the clutches of hysteria. You will be allowed to talk, think, and dream of nothing else until it's over. Your relationship will be transformed into a business partnership, focused on task delegation, conflict management, and crisis assessment.

I ran into an old friend not too long ago. He and his girlfriend dated for six years, living together for three of them, before he proposed. It was a great relationship—easy and fun. But after getting engaged, they found themselves having screaming matches in a crowded department store about which china pattern to choose. He looked shell-shocked and scared. I could offer little comfort beyond "This too shall pass. Also: Can you push up the date?"

One couple, Deborah and Ari, did just that. In less than seven months they moved from being casual friends to close companions to a serious couple planning a future together. They were both in their thirties, knew what they wanted, and recognized what they'd found in each other. There didn't seem to be a reason to wait.

They got engaged in mid-February and set a date of April 1. Ten weeks. People asked if she was pregnant. She wasn't. She was just smart. And valued her mental health.

They pulled off a gorgeous wedding: Ceremony in a park, reception in a quirky museum. There was good music and great food, a pretty dress, and whimsical table numbers. They even created a picture collage in their spare time. I'm sure a few guests couldn't make it because of preexisting plans. And it was definitely a busy couple of months for Deborah and Ari. But then it was over!

It's a choice: You can opt to stretch things out and agonize over tiny details for months, or you can put yourself on a time-table that forces you to make decisions and move on with your life. I've seen what happens to couples who are engaged for two years or more. By the time they reach the wedding, they've near-alienated many of their loved ones. They sometimes no longer recognize themselves or even particularly like each other. It's ugly. And with a $50 billion wedding industry that bets on you feeling the planning pressure, things aren't likely to change anytime soon.

So do what you can to save yourself: Keep a box of wine in the fridge. Try to stay off the blogs. Set a date for sooner rather than later.

And don't let them see you cry.

Godspeed.

How to Get Married Without Losing Friends or Alienating People

My wedding wish for you is twofold. One: I hope that when it's all over, you will be legally married to your favorite person on earth. If you've accomplished that, you have succeeded. Two: I hope that all your dearest friends and relatives haven't come to resent you by the time you cut the cake. If the latter is a goal you happen to share, here are some tips to keep in mind:

1. Your loved ones will want to be involved with your blessed day and help in whatever way possible. Except by refereeing fights over guest lists, registries, wedding bands, seating charts, or appetizer options. That is on you.

2. Please don't feel like you have to keep everyone updated on your progress or stress levels via daily updates on Facebook. They'll be able to live with the suspense.

3. Over the course of your engagement, your friends will occasionally want to talk about something other than the wedding. In order to facilitate this, it's advisable to posit the following questions: "So, how are you?" "What's happening in your world?"

4. As requested, many guests will save the date of your wedding. They may not, however, save the dates of multiple engagement parties; your bachelor or bachelorette weekend; the first, second, and third shower; the rehearsal dinner or morning-after brunch. Again: Keep. It. Short.

5. Do not make your guests wait thirty or more minutes for the ceremony to start. If the invite said 5 P.M., the masses will get restless by 5:15.

6. No tongue at the altar. Please?

7. If possible, try not to book your ceremony and reception a stressful sixty-mile drive away from each other. Also, please try to avoid scheduling a five hour gap between them. If this cannot be accomplished, be prepared for your guests to show up half drunk. They had to kill the time somehow.

8. It's wonderful that you are a gluten-free, dairy-free, raw-food-eating, vegan locavore. But your guests may not be.

Don't be offended if they duck out in search of a nearby McDonald's.

9. If you are happy and enjoying yourself, your loved ones will be, too. If you are overwrought and yelling at the event manager for arranging the floating candles wrong, they will notice. You set the tone. Everyone else will follow your lead.

Pre-Party

When I follow up with couples after their weddings I always ask about the emotional highlight of their day.

Almost invariably they say it was the ceremony—and usually they say that with a note of surprise. Sometimes they'll talk about the instant their eyes first met from opposite ends of the aisle, and how for a second it seemed like they were the only two people in the universe. Or they'll tell me how, in the midst of their vows, a voice cracked or one of them fumbled their words and the solemnity was broken by laughter. Or they'll describe the moment when they looked out and saw all the people they loved most in the world sitting together, looking back at them.

There is magic in the ceremony. At the end of it, you are fundamentally different than you were at the beginning. Although what transpires there can be revoked, it can never be fully undone.

The wedding industry places so much focus on the reception—picking the perfect linens, the best deejay, the right signature cocktail—that the ceremony often gets overlooked. But it's one of the few momentous occasions in life that you can actually plan for, so you might as well give it some thought. (Chances are you won't have the same opportunity with your funeral.)

Religions differ when it comes to how much you can personalize a wedding ceremony. But there seems to be room in all of them to make the ritual specific to you. You can do that with a reading or a song or—and I promise I have seen this—an interpretive dance. Maybe all the children in attendance walk down the aisle before you. Or you have a close friend say a few words about how you fit together as a couple. You could ask your guests to pass the rings from person to person, offering a silent blessing before you finally present them to each other, or you might write personalized vows that are tender and hilarious.

Whatever. Just spend some fraction of the time you use mulling transportation and hors d'oeuvre options to think about what you want from the ceremony itself. That doesn't mean it has to be groundbreaking, or to stretch over an hour. (I'm pretty sure ours did, but that's because I'm ridiculous and demanded that the ceremony include almost all my favorite elements from each of the hundreds of weddings I'd seen. We did, at least, give our guests the chance to grab some spiked cider before they sat down.)

Everyone will tell you that your wedding day goes by in a flash. And that's true. But time can stand still when you're at the altar or under the chuppah. Make sure that moment—one that will be crystalline in your minds forever—is exactly what you want it to be.

Toasts

Here is the goal: short, sincere, short.

For my sister's wedding in Pittsburgh a decade ago, my father and I both prepared elaborate speeches. We wanted to make the guests laugh and cry and wave their napkins in outbursts of delight.

After finishing our long toasts, the best man got up and this is what he said: "Pitt won today. You guys are great. Go, Steelers."

Guess who got the standing ovation?

Like I said—keep it short.

Ban the Chicken Dance

Having spent what sometimes seems like half my life at other people's weddings, I feel qualified to propose a few improvements to the ritual, like making the following traditions illegal:

Receiving lines: This is not Space Mountain. Do your guests really have to queue up just to get the chance to talk to you? Maybe just wait to chat until everyone's had the chance to get some champagne.

Bride's side/Groom's side: Come on, ye Montagues and Capulets. Must guests really choose an allegiance?

Bridal parties being forced to enter the reception as if they are trying out for *Soul Train:* At best there will be two members of the group who can actually dance. Everyone else looks like they want to die. So do the guests being forced to watch this debacle.

Bridal parties in general: I have never figured out the purpose of the bridal party. Is there something you need done that can only be executed by people in matching outfits? The numbers never work out, so you're always either hurting one person's feelings or recruiting someone extraneous into service. Of course I get that you want to honor your closest friends, but I think there must be a way to do this that doesn't involve them using half a paycheck for the honor of wearing an unflattering outfit of your choosing.

Glass clinking to prompt a kiss: Drunk, elderly uncles and freckle-faced ten-year-old cousins—the demographics who are the biggest proponents of this tradition—are probably not reading this book. But you have a choice! Just ignore them and soon enough they'll go back to annoying the people at their own table.

Bouquet toss: I promise you, the wedding has already been awkward enough for your single female friends. There is no need to line them up for inspection and then test their athletic ability by having them scramble over one another to snatch up your wilting bouquet. You keep your flowers; they keep their dignity.

Anything having to do with a garter belt: Just, no.

Toasts that rhyme: Or are given by three or more people passing one sheet of paper back and forth. Come on, ladies. (Unfortunately this public speaking crime is almost always committed by ladies.) We can do better than that.

Cake smashing: This reveals a *little* too much about the complexity of your feelings for each other. Of course there will be times when you want to aggressively rub your beloved's face in something, probably much less pleasant than cake. Now is not the time. Just for today let your guests believe in your fairy tale.

The wedding favor: Unless it's a cookie, it's getting tossed as soon as we walk out the door. So save your money, save the earth and spare your guests the guilt of chucking that miniature framed photo of the two of you.

The elaborate sendoff: You made your guests leave the dance floor twenty minutes early so a bossy wedding planner could arrange them near the exit with sparklers to usher you off into the night? But you're all going back to the same hotel bar after! If you absolutely must capture this manufactured moment, consider using the catering staff as stand-ins while your guests finish their drinks.

The Good Stuff

People always ask me if I'm sick of weddings, and the previous chapter might have made it seem that way. The truth is, I'm not. Yes, sometimes it's wearing to get dressed up week after week and to miss out on other fun Saturday night shenanigans with my friends and family. But once I'm there, seated among strangers, waiting for the couple to make their way down the aisle, I always feel lucky to have a job that allows me to witness a collection of tender moments.

Nothing beats watching a groom's eyes well up with tears when he sees his bride in her wedding dress for the first time. Or catching the look a father gives his daughter just before the doors to the church open. I love it when weddings happen in the midst of a downpour or a blizzard. When a group of people, who may not have known one another before this day, are all suddenly best friends, united in love for the couple they've come to celebrate.

I love the sweetness of little kids twirling with their parents during the dinner hour when no one else is on the dance floor. I love it when people surprise themselves by crying during toasts and when grandparents beam from the sidelines, blessed to see their baby's baby all grown up.

This is the wonder of weddings—the little things that add up to something miraculous. Whether they're fancy or simple, large or small, weddings are a testament to hope and love and an enduring belief in the world's goodness.

It's all right there, compressed in the promise of those tiny words: I do.

MAKING IT LAST

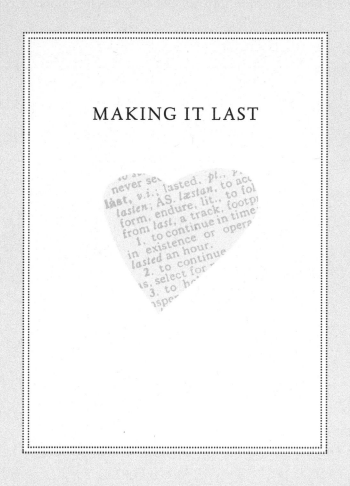

Here is the single most important thing I discovered during my years of writing about relationships: You can learn to be good at them. In fact, you have to be willing to learn, in order to be good at them.

Because it is not intuitive. Not all of it, and not for everyone. Not even for you, Dr. Phil.

Falling in love requires little forethought. You can put yourself in the position to meet somebody, but ultimately you have about as much control over it as you have over sneezing. That's why they call it falling—it's involuntary, scary, and exhilarating. And we often expect what follows to be similarly effortless. You came to love this person so easily. Why should maintaining that affection be any different?

I'm not sure, really. Maybe evolution only provides us with the tools to make babies, not to look at the same, increasingly wrinkled face across the breakfast table every morning for decades.

Of course, we know that relationships change when the first blush of infatuation starts to fade. We just don't like it. We certainly don't like the thought of having to do something in order to sustain a gift that seemed to magically drop into our laps from the heavens. Because then it doesn't seem like magic anymore. We're forced to concede that what we have is earthly, imperfect, and fragile.

Actively setting out to learn about relationships seems like the least romantic thing imaginable. Shameful, even. Better keep that stack of self-help books hidden from view—and whatever you do, don't admit it when things aren't working and you need help.

But there is an even less romantic alternative: doing nothing and letting the priceless love you've been given wither as you hold fast to the idea that once you've found "the one," everything else should just fall into place. And then deciding that if the relationship isn't living up to your fantasy, it must mean you didn't marry the right person after all. It's no surprise that our national divorce rate is almost 50 percent.

Trying to get better at relationships requires a shift in perspective—a new sense of curiosity. What components contribute to a relationship's success or failure? What behaviors help it along? What patterns, needs, or expectations do we consistently bring to the table in our own unique partnerships?

The good news: There are many people who are very smart about these issues and huge reserves of resources waiting to guide us. We can read the books or take a communication course, find a good counselor, go on a relationship retreat, or talk to people whose marriages we admire. "Pick the right person" is an important piece of advice; but it isn't the only one.

I felt lucky, going into my marriage, that I'd had the benefit of learn-

ing so much from so many people. They'd taught me a little about what to expect and a lot about how one should endeavor to behave in a close relationship.

Mostly they taught me that there is almost always help—and wisdom—available. About a month after we started dating, Aaron and I had a conversation that seemed both premature and absolutely pressing. He told me it was important to him to raise Jewish children. I said it was important to me to raise kids who have a close relationship with God. Those things didn't seem mutually exclusive, and so we went on our merry way, feeling confident we had that little issue all figured out.

Except that then there was the question of Christmas trees . . . and parental expectations . . . and, you know, our own actual beliefs. It became abundantly clear that we had a long way to go. We muddled through for a while, alternating between frustration and denial, before admitting that we needed help.

Together we enrolled in two eight-week-long workshops for interfaith couples. The courses were guided by a very cool rabbi and they gave us the chance to meet other couples grappling with the same issues we were. We could compare notes and learn from one another. At times it felt awkward and intense, but Aaron and I came away from each session feeling like we understood each other better and had a more solid plan for the future.

No one person or course or book could ever reveal everything there is to know about relationships—and certainly not about your particular relationship. But maybe as you read these stories you'll glean from them, as I did, a few interesting insights or useful tips about how to navigate *this strange territory known as marriage. Perhaps you'll simply come away with a slightly altered attitude or a little fresh hope and that will be enough.*

I promise that the lessons of these wise people won't diminish the magic of love. And if we're lucky, they might help sustain it.

Ever After

Recently my four-year-old niece and I watched the Disney animated film *Cinderella*. Well, I watched it, anyway; she got bored and went outside to play.

When the credits started to roll, I felt a little cheated. The movie wrapped up so quickly. I'd invested my entire morning with sweet Cinderelly, watching her scrub the floors and wash the dishes and fend off that mean old cat and evil stepmother. But once the glass slipper fits, that's it! Cinderella and her prince don't share so much as a cup of tea—never mind a proper heart-to-heart—before the storybook flips to the last page. "And They Lived Happily Ever After."

Perhaps it's best that my niece left the room. Not because of the look-pretty-and-be-rescued-by-a-prince moral of the story; she's smart enough and tough enough to see through that one. What's more insidious is the idea that finding a mate somehow rescues us from ourselves. That once we pair off with the right partner, the drudgery of our former lives will instantly vanish. We'll be validated and whole—and no longer required to pay taxes, visit the DMV, or watch what we eat. Or, at least in Cinderella's case, clean the floors.

Does it go without saying that there's actually no such thing as Happily Ever After? That life generally acquires new ripples of complication and angst once you walk down the aisle, apply for a thirty-year mortgage, and have a few children?

Of course a loving relationship adds great sweetness to life. That's why most of us want one. And, as we're often reminded, people in happy marriages tend to live longer and be more financially stable. But no one's struggles are erased the minute they partner up. Committed relationships come with their own challenges—learning to compromise, honoring someone else's needs as much as your own, tolerating another person in your space when all you want is ten minutes alone.

And that's just the start. Then come the major life stressors: ailing family members, financial crisis, fertility issues, children with special needs. These challenges have destroyed more marriages than anyone could count.

And all of this is layered on top of your own issues. Whatever baggage you were already carrying when you met Mr. or Ms. Right comes with you into the relationship. If you had depressive tendencies before, you will certainly have them again. If you struggled with addiction or an eating disorder or low self-esteem or high anxiety, you will continue to grapple with it after saying "I do." The problem may even be amplified under your partner's watchful eye.

The point is that life never gets easy. But if we can accept that there will always be challenges and hard times intermixed with the beauty and joy, then we won't be so disappointed when the difficult moments come around. When we're feeling particularly evolved, we might even tell ourselves that the tough stuff is usually also the good stuff—unparalleled opportunities for growth—just temporarily disguised.

I'm glad Cinderella found her prince and had what appeared to be a hell of a wedding. And I hope the memory of that day helped sustain her when she wanted to throttle Mr. Charming for leaving his laundry out and she found herself cleaning floors once again. The truth is, the last line of their story should probably be changed to "Happily Ever After— Except When They Were Sad or Bored or Tired, Which Did Happen on Occasion, but Didn't Make Their Life Together Any Less Beautiful."

That's an ending I can believe in.

Check Your Expectations

You know that thing that happens when everyone keeps telling you how phenomenal a movie is, and that you absolutely *must* see it, and then you do and you're like, *"Meh, it was fine. A little overhyped"*? But you also know that if it hadn't been pumped up so much, you probably would have thought it was pretty great?

We've done precisely that to marriage, and set ourselves up for a letdown.

Diane Solee is the wild-haired queen of the marriage education movement. By the time we met she was in her mid-sixties, but still bubbling with drive and energy. It had been thirty years since her husband, the father of her two sons, asked for a divorce; thirty years since she crawled under her dining room table, assumed the fetal position, and bawled.

Ironically, the split didn't sour her on marriage. Instead it turned her into the institution's fiercest advocate. I was just a few months past my own breakup when we sat down at the kitchen table of her comfortable white stucco home for an interview. She asked me almost as many questions about my personal life as I asked about her professional expertise. *Yes, I was single. No, I didn't think I should get back together with my ex. Sure, I was starting to date again, but so far no one special.*

When I finally stood to leave after a three-hour interview, she suggested I use the restroom. I told her I was fine.

"No! You have to go before you drive home," she insisted, ushering me in. "I want you to go!" Then she cried through the closed door, "And I want you to get *married*!"

One thing at a time, I told her.

Diane's main message is threefold: 1) Marriage is good. Life is richer and easier when you go through it with a partner. 2) Couples need to learn skills—how to fight, how to compromise, how to forgive—in order to be good at marriage. 3) Our expectations of marriage are way out of whack.

We've been duped, she told me, by love songs and big-screen romances and the myth "that it's about finding the right person—that if you find your soul mate, everything will be fine."

To understand what she means, it's helpful to briefly review the history of marriage. Once upon a time women were traded for cattle and marriages were arranged by village elders and usually people had no say in who they married, but that was okay because as long as the union produced a few sturdy new farmhands it was considered a grand success. Except "once upon a time" was not so long ago—this was more or less the case through much of human existence. As Stephanie Coontz writes in her definitive *Marriage, a History: How Love Conquered Marriage,* marriages were long considered far too important to "be entered into solely on the basis of something as irrational as love."

"Marriage," she argues, "was not primarily about the individual needs and desires of a man and a woman and the children they produced. Marriage had as much to do with getting good in-laws and increasing one's family labor force as it did with finding a lifetime companion and raising a beloved child."

Not that our forebears shunned romance. "People have always loved a love story," Coontz writes. "But for most of the past, our ancestors did not try to live in one."

For thousands of years love was thought to be crazy-making and even dangerous. It was more likely to damage a marriage than bolster it. That only changed a couple of centuries ago, during the Age of Enlightenment, when people started to choose their own spouses. Without such strong ties to the land, folks began to worry as much about their emotional needs as they did about harvesting next year's crop. Love matches came into vogue and marriage continued to evolve with the dawn of women's rights and the increasing availability of divorce.

Which lands us where we are today. It is rare to encounter someone in the United States who has married for any reason *other* than love. Even more interesting is how thoroughly optional marriage, or even domestic partnership, has become. It's no longer necessary for economic survival or access to sex or the chance to have and raise children. All the single ladies—and gents—can manage on their own.

But here's the rub: Though we need marriage less today, we expect more from it.

Now we don't just want a marriage to be stable. We also want it to be satisfying, passionate, and occasionally thrilling. We expect total sexual fulfillment and demand absolute monogamy. We want undying love and we want the bills paid, the laundry folded, and the kids in bed by 9 P.M.

So even as Diane Sollee works to build marriage up, she's also trying to take it down a notch. She wants couples who are getting ready to walk down the aisle to know—*really know*—that it will be hard. That there will be times when one or both of them want out and can barely stand the sight of each other. That they'll be bored, then frustrated, angry, and perhaps resentful. And that it will be particularly tough at first . . . and then it will be particularly tough again when they have teenagers . . . and again when the teenagers leave and it's just the two of them and they realize they don't really know what to say to each other in the new silence.

Diane also wants them to know that all of these things are normal. Because maybe if they know what to expect, they'll have the fortitude to see their marriage through the rough times and focus on the positive—the life they've built together, the love they share, the comfort they've given each other and come home to.

Maybe occasionally they'll even think it's all worth it—the good, the bad, and the boring. And they'll be grateful that Hollywood got it wrong. Because the big screen almost never does justice to the richness of reality.

Past Romance

Chris and Evelyn were one of the first couples I fell in love with.

He first spotted her at a crowded party in 1942. Chris took one look at this young woman with chic bangs and thought, "There's the girl for me." Evelyn told him she was engaged to another man, but Chris still found a way to walk her home. They stopped at a burger joint on the way and he ordered an onions-only sandwich just to make her laugh.

Evelyn quickly called things off with the other guy. She married Chris two months later. Then he shipped off to the Pacific. His first deployment lasted forty days; the next one spanned two years. During both, Evelyn wrote him a letter *every single day*. Chris lost his wallet once overseas, but miraculously got it back. It contained his prized possession: twenty photos of Evelyn.

After the war came five children, a home in the D.C. suburbs, and Chris's long career with the CIA. Soon enough
there were thirteen grandchildren, a retirement in Florida,
and then his stroke, which forced them to move back to Virginia. When I met them the two were in an apartment at a
senior living center. At eighty-six Chris was sarcastic and
strong, but tears formed in his eyes when he talked about how
Evelyn had sustained him over the sixty-five years they'd been
married.

At the end of the interview, I asked Chris if he liked living
in the retirement community—it was a nice enough place, as
these things go, the kind that smells like fresh-baked cookies
and always has someone playing show tunes on the lobby
piano.

"Not really," he said flatly. "But that's okay," he added,
looking at Evelyn. "I like you, kid."

I walked away wishing I were their fourteenth grandchild.
But more than that, I envied their generation. It just seemed
like they knew how to do relationships—you fell in love, got
married, and stuck with the partnership. Through good times
and bad. There was none of the angst and hand-wringing that
defines most twenty-first-century love lives.

Later, I mentioned my jealousy to Barry McCarthy, a very
wise psychologist who has written several books about relationships and had been practicing couples counseling for almost four decades.

"No, no, no, no, no, no, no," McCarthy said, tapping his fingers together. "We don't want to go back to the way it was." Maybe the divorce rate was lower fifty years ago, he told me, but the marital satisfaction rate was almost certainly lower, as well. People were stuck in bad marriages, even in cases of alcoholism or abuse.

Most relationships today actually are better off than their counterparts a few decades ago, McCarthy explained, although it might not be obvious at first glance. Partners now talk about issues more openly and are increasingly likely to seek help in times of trouble.

I thought about how many stories I'd read of couples celebrating their sixtieth or seventieth anniversaries, or dying within hours of each other after a lifetime together. And then I thought of how many stories I hadn't read . . . about miserable marriages, adultery, or divorce. We don't like stories like that, so they usually don't get written.

McCarthy is probably right—romanticizing the past won't help us with the future.

It's easy to idealize our parents or grandparents when they seem to have it all figured out. And maybe they do—but they might fail to mention how many tears or screaming matches or nights on the couch it took to get them to where they are.

My conversation with Barry McCarthy didn't make me love Chris and Evelyn less. If anything, I admired them more.

I realized they had probably struggled in ways I could never imagine, perhaps with issues they'd never discussed with anyone.

And they were still together, smiling at each other through it all.

Sometimes You're Miserable?
Good. That's Normal.

My favorite scene from Iris Krasnow's delicious, insightful book, *The Secret Lives of Wives*, comes at the beginning of the second chapter. Iris, then the mother of four boys under the age of four (including a set of twins), is wearing a gray bathrobe splattered with "poop, milk and smashed organic peas." After her husband has eaten a breakfast that Iris made, treated himself to a nice cup of coffee and left for work, she straps her twins into a hands-free breastfeeding contraption and begins to vacuum.

Then she catches a glimpse of her haggard self in the mirror, bursts into tears, and comes to a decision: She will get a divorce. She's already doing everything around the house—who needs that guy? Iris's mother helpfully supports her plan, saying, "I never liked him anyways."

In the end, Iris didn't toss her marriage out the window. (And her mother eventually retracted those words and would swear she'd always adored her son-in-law.) But though her thought, happily, was a fleeting one, versions of it would still cross her mind from time to time. So years later, as Iris prepared to become an empty-nester, she set out to understand what allows some couples to actually keep the vows, "till death do we part." In compiling *The Secret Lives of Wives,* she interviewed hundreds of women, asking how they maintained their sanity and sense of self and some tiny thread of love over a lifetime with one person. Some said they took separate vacations or poured themselves into creative pursuits. Others had friends—male and female—who offered the kind of companionship their husbands could not. A few had liaisons on the side.

When I met Iris after her book was released, she told me the biggest commonality among women who were still satisfied with their marriages after decades together was that they "never bought into the dangerous fantasy—the myth—of Happily Ever After." The collective wisdom seems to be: "Sometimes you will be miserable. This is the reality of long-term intimacy. Carry on."

Isn't it nice to know that it's perfectly fine to want to stab your partner in the eye once in a while? Or to dream of running off to Mexico with the pool boy? Or to actually run off to Mexico for a monthlong photography workshop just to remind yourself of who you are? That it's all part of the bargain and doesn't indicate a broken marriage?

"A long marriage takes guts, humility and constant work,"

Iris writes. And she counts herself among those who are still happy in their totally imperfect, often infuriating, occasionally miserable marriages. So what has kept her in a twenty-six-year marriage and away from acting on any temptation to flee?

Iris says that it was the advice she got years ago from a girlfriend who happens to be a sex therapist. The friend offered three words of wisdom that have become Iris's go-to refrain for young people looking for marriage advice: "Lower your expectations."

When you're prepared for some moments of misery, you'll be better able to withstand the storms that are inevitable in any marriage—and more likely to reach the rainbow on the other side.

Bearing Witness

It's always seemed to me that being in a relationship is, in large part, about bearing witness. You take a front-row seat to your partner's daily trials and triumphs and they do the same for you. And then at the end of your life at least one person knows what you went through—how often you struggled, how hard you tried, and how much goodness you created.

I once wrote a story about two young people with severe mental disabilities who fell in love. It was a purer love than almost any I've encountered. Bill and Shelley met at a social club for teens with special needs. He had Down syndrome. Shelley, born with excessive fluid in her brain, had repeatedly surprised the doctors who'd told her parents she wouldn't live past infancy.

Bill was twelve when they first laid eyes on each other. Shelley was a pretty, petite brunette with a couple of years on him, but Bill made a move anyway. "I didn't know what love was until I met her," he told me. Friendship blossomed to romance and eventually he took her to his junior and senior prom. Bill even told Shelley's parents he'd convert to Judaism to be with her. But after high school they lost touch.

About a decade later, however, they both signed up for a program that takes people with developmental disabilities on cruises. And when Shelley got seasick, it was Bill who volunteered to take care of her.

"I want to be Shelley's hero," he told me later. "I want to be her avenger."

Soon they were meeting regularly for dinners and outings. After a few months, Bill asked Shelley to marry him, presenting her with a ruby ring bought with savings from his job at a grocery store.

At first, Bill's and Shelley's parents had reservations about what marriage would look like for the two. Before marrying, the couple moved into an assisted-living apartment together and started attending weekly sessions with a counselor. They worked on communication skills and learned to be responsive to each other's needs and boundaries. They played board games, made up puns, traveled with each other's families, and developed a social calendar packed with social events and activities.

And they loved each other completely. "When I see her

she's like a bright penny," Bill told me. "She's like the color orange, like a real joyful, lively spirit. Her love is like pink. There is so much good in her that I really fell in love with."

After living together for two years, their families finally consented to a wedding.

When I sat down with Shelley's parents, the big day was quickly approaching. Her mother said they'd fought hard to give Shelley the best life possible, but hadn't been able to fill a fundamental gap. For years, until she reunited with Bill, Shelley had been lonely. Her father was almost silent until the end of our interview, when I asked what it was like to see their daughter getting married. Then he started to cry.

"You want your children to be happy," he said. "Having a mate—someone who really cares if you come home at night, someone who cares whether you're well or sick—that makes life worthwhile."

Zen teacher John Tarrant once said, "Attention is the most basic form of love." Why do babies cry and dogs scratch at our legs? They want attention. They want love. (Unless it's breakfast and you're having bacon. Then they just want bacon.)

For one story I interviewed a woman whose life had fallen apart before it improved. For years Kalena led a whirling existence in New York City—she ate at great restaurants, did a little modeling, and started her own online media company, which quickly put her on national lists of "ones to watch." She married, made lots of money, and traveled extensively.

But before long the marriage began to crack. Around the same time her father died; then her mother became gravely ill, compelling Kalena to take in her two younger brothers, then just in middle school.

It was all she could do to stay afloat as she started a new life in Washington, D.C., as a divorcée and guardian of two struggling teens. But she never let anyone see behind her beautiful, stoic veneer. An assistant principal at one of the boys' schools could see through it, however. It was obvious to Ben that Kalena's brother—and the whole family—was in pain. He took the boy under his wing and coached Kalena on how to help him cope. As they met to talk about her brother, a mutual attraction grew, though Kalena dismissed it. She was determined not to be hurt again.

But Ben kept coming around. He kept listening. He was there when her mother died. When Kalena stood up to give a eulogy at the funeral, he was front and center. And afterward, he told her that her speech had been lovely, but lacking. She'd never mentioned her own feelings. "I'm definitely good at smiling through things," Kalena told me. "Nobody wants to know all these horrible things in your life. So the fact that he saw that—I felt like he saw me." After that conversation she told him for the first time that she loved him. Ten months later they were married.

Paying attention takes time and focus—two things we're

short on these days. Sitting next to each other while surfing the Web on separate laptops doesn't cut it. Neither does dinner if your eyes are on your cellphone as much as they're on your partner. A neglected spouse might not clamor for your attention as aggressively as a pet, but they need the dose of love just as much.

Terri Orbuch, a sociology professor at the University of Michigan, Oakland, has conducted one of the nation's most extensive studies of couples—373 pairs over twenty years. She learned which behaviors lead to happy unions and which ones often spell divorce.

One of the practices Orbuch promotes most fervently is what she calls the "ten-minute rule": For ten minutes each day, couples should "talk about something other than work, family, who does what around the house or your relationship." The goal is "to always really understand your partner." To not lose sight of their goals and dreams and passions—the things that probably drew you to them in the first place. As you share breakfast in the morning or wind down before bed, the rule offers a chance to talk about your partner's wish list of vacation destinations or about a book they're reading. Anything that allows you to stop and connect and not just feel like business partners trying to make your way through a packed agenda.

A groom once admitted to me, a week before his wedding, that he was still learning about his bride. They'd been together for almost five years at that point, so it wasn't a shotgun wedding. But over the course of their relationship, he'd found that there were always corners of her mind, aspects of her personality and facts about her life that popped up as new revelations.

"I'll probably keep learning about her for the rest of my life," he told me.

We should all be so lucky. Ten minutes of conversation. That's nothing. And it's not hard. It just requires us to briefly pause and see—*really see*—the person with whom we're sharing a life.

Acceptance

Once I wrote about the time when God got married . . . to God. At least, that's how the two very human-looking people at the altar explained it.

The couple, both mind-body healers and metaphysical authors who meditated for several hours a day, had, they said, reached enlightenment. Lisa and Rick first met years earlier when she brought a troubled nephew to see him. She became Rick's student and then, when his first marriage ended, his romantic partner.

"It's joy," Lisa told me of their relationship. "It's just like a fountain of joy coming into every aspect of life—this sweet, sweet joy."

Her groom, Rick, elaborated. "You are a soul and you have a mind and you have a body, but those are just mere extensions of what you are, which is the Divine. And you're with another person who also has that and you are in love with each other and you make love with each other as two souls who are one and have these extensions of mind and body. And you have the bliss of being one in God at the same time as you're coming together in each other."

That's how it is for you, too, right?

I tell this story because that was the only time I wrote about God getting married to God; the rest of us, unfortunately, are apparently consigned to mortals. Our partners are always late. Or they're always twenty minutes early and insist that you be, too. They never wash their own dishes. Unless they're constantly after you to clean up your crap. They pick their nose in the kitchen, forget to fill up the gas tank, and have the nerve to complain when you buy the wrong brand of toothpaste.

And the worst part is that you can't change them. A study by two psychologists in New Zealand, Shreena Hira and Nickola Overall, found that when people tried to improve their relationships by changing their spouse, the romances actually got worse. "Relationship improvement attempts that target the partner may generally be ineffective because partners react negatively and are not receptive to change," wrote the authors. (Read: Nagging doesn't work.)

But, interestingly, Hira and Overall also found that there wasn't much more relationship satisfaction when people focused on self-improvement, either. The only thing that really seemed to help was seeing a partner making changes on their own. But people have to really *want* to change their behavior before they're able to do so.

That usually leaves only one possibility: Accept As Is. (Unless "As Is" includes abuse or addiction.)

I invited psychologist Christine Meinecke to do an online chat after reading her brilliantly titled book, *Everybody Marries the Wrong Person.* Meinecke's premise is that we're doing ourselves a real disservice by believing there's such a thing as the *right* person. She says the only road to marital bliss passes through the land of acceptance. When one reader asked her when to voice complaints and when to keep the peace, Meinecke responded, "The key is to understand that partners are not renovation projects. Think always in terms of looking at your own expectations, negative emotional responses, dark moods and insecurities and deal with them first."

John Gottman refers to the problem as the "if onlies": "If only she was a little better with money . . ."; "If only he didn't spend so much time watching sports . . ." You can keep hoping, but the truth is that you're arguing against reality. And that's an argument you will lose. He watches a lot of sports. She is how she is with money. The more you rail against these things, the more frustrated you'll both become.

One of my wisest editors at the *Post,* a woman who lost her husband to cancer when her twin sons were still in grade school, told me that the lyrics of the Don Henley song "For My Wedding" reflect her hope for every young person getting married:

To want what I have
To take what I'm given with grace.

It's hard to be happy with what you have when you're busy wishing for something different. But no one knows how much time they'll get with their perfectly imperfect partner. So focus on loving them, just as they are.

Winning Isn't Everything

I'm a master deflector, as my friends will tell you. If they ask me a question, I'll soon steer the conversation back to their lives. Sometimes I get points for being a good listener, but really it's just a shy girl's coping mechanism of choice. So I immediately started to sweat when I arrived at a brunch hosted by a group of women who read my wedding column religiously. All were in their fifties and sixties, some perpetually single, others divorced, one married for decades. While I knew they'd organized the event to hear from me, I quickly turned the tables on them, asking them about their stories. And of course, they were fascinating.

I asked the no-nonsense woman who'd been married longest, more than thirty years, for her secret. I'll never forget the answer she gave in her deep, husky voice: Don't escalate. At the beginning of her relationship, she explained, she was inclined to amplify every argument. Each issue seemed like a big deal and it was an even bigger deal to establish the clear supe-riority of whatever position she happened to hold. Of course, she sighed, that got exhausting. Eventually she realized she didn't always have to dig in. She could let things go—even if it meant not getting her way—and life would go on. In fact, it would usually continue more serenely than it had before.

I've heard similar advice dozens of times since meeting that very wise woman. Usually it's wrapped in the cliché "You can be right, or you can be married." This is one of those tru-isms that make a great deal of logical sense but are hard to put into practice. Counselors, however, are increasingly urging couples to stop thinking about who's right and who's wrong in favor of a different question: "What's best for the relation-ship?"

When psychologists from UCLA studied the attitudes and behaviors of 172 couples during their first eleven years of marriage, they found that people who had a deeper commit-ment to the health of their relationships than to their own personal agendas were more likely to remain happily married. Obviously this meant those people had to sometimes be will-ing to give up the outcome they wanted—even on issues that mattered deeply to them—but they knew the benefit of such a sacrifice would outweigh its personal cost.

Another study, led by Eli J. Finkel of Northwestern Univer-sity, tracked the satisfaction of 120 couples over the course of two years. Every three months, half of the participants com-pleted a writing assignment that asked them to consider the last major disagreement they had with their partner from the perspective of a neutral third party supportive of the relationship. The other half had no such assignment. Finkel and his colleagues found that those couples who did the writing assignments were not only more satisfied overall, but also had greater levels of sexual desire and passion. They thrived with a wider perspective. Crucially, though, the study showed that the happier couples still fought—and in fact fought about weighty problems—but weren't as distressed by the arguments. It was easier for them to remember that they were on the same team, working together toward shared goals.

The scholar Joseph Campbell once wrote that "marriage is not a simple love affair, it's an ordeal, and the ordeal is the sacrifice of ego to a relationship in which two have become one."

Still, I think sometimes you can be married *and* be right. You just don't have to tell your partner about it.

But Don't Turn Away
from the Dark Side

One of the saddest interviews I've ever conducted was with a woman in the midst of a divorce that she desperately wished wasn't happening.

She and her husband had been together for almost twenty years. They had four children. She'd seen him through serious illnesses and the stresses of running a busy household. Her parents had been married for decades and she always assumed that's how her life would be, as well. Even when the woman found that she and her husband could only discuss serious topics and points of contention via email, she never doubted their marriage would improve, and survive.

Then one afternoon she was served with separation papers. "I almost had a heart attack," she recalled of the shock.

She told no one what had happened and vowed to do everything she could to save the marriage—make his favorite dinners, be a better wife, go to counseling. Nothing worked.

And as the divorce proceeded, she discovered she didn't know her husband as well as she'd thought.

And there was much she'd been unwilling to acknowledge. In her family, she was known as saintly. She loved babies and old people and would do anything for anyone. She was a peacemaker who cried easily and loathed conflict. Those qualities had served her well in many aspects of life, but might have left her ill-prepared to face the darker moments in marriage.

"My parents made it look so easy, which is good," she told me. "But you have to learn how to work through issues. You can't just put things under a blanket and pretend they don't exist. How do you do that if you're not taught that? If you're not raised that way?"

I always like talking to couples who are walking down the aisle for a second or third time. For one thing, their enduring belief in love is impressive. And usually their approach to marriage is a little different from that of starry-eyed first-timers. They've learned the hard way what doesn't work and are always determined that things will be different this time around.

When I ask what makes them think that the new marriage will be a success, some of them say they're *sure* they've found the right person this time. But the more convincing ones talk about *becoming* the right person. And almost inevitably they say that the biggest mistake they made in their previous relationship was letting problems build or pushing them under the rug. That worked only until one of them couldn't take it anymore and had to get out.

Nobody likes admitting there are serious troubles in their marriage, but ignoring them won't make things any better. Usually they end up getting a lot worse. We're not talking about petty complaints here—putting the toilet paper roll on wrong or stealing the covers in the middle of the night. It's when consequential concerns—addiction, adultery, sexual dysfunction, communication issues or emotional distance—are left to fester that even relationships that started out blissfully will begin to rot.

And it's not just the marriage that's endangered. Studies have shown that people in unhappy marriages have an increased risk for serious diseases including cancer, diabetes, heart disease, and arthritis.

Regina DeMeo was a Washington, D.C., divorce lawyer for seven years before she went through a divorce herself. Like most people, the petite, dark-haired beauty never thought it would happen to her. But after it did, she became committed to helping others build better relationships and—if divorce was inevitable—to separate more civilly through the process of mediation.

"If you can save this marriage, that's what you should try to do," she recalled telling clients when we met in the lobby of an old D.C. hotel. "Because I can tell you personally, I've been down this dark path, and it's not fun."

In a recent essay, DeMeo estimates that 75 percent of the

people who come to see her wanting a divorce first saw a relationship counselor. Why didn't it help? "The answer is simple," she writes. "They waited too long. When too much damage has been done to a relationship, there comes a point where you just can't turn back and undo all those little acts that on their own might have seemed minor, yet when put together, grossly tipped the scales in favor of getting out and ending the pain, rather than staying in and risking further injury to your ego or mental health."

Elizabeth Weil is a writer who spent a year trying to improve her already fine marriage. She dragged her husband to relationship workshops, sex coaching, religious counseling, and therapy sessions. In the end, she concluded that the added attention to their marriage was beneficial, even as she came to appreciate the idiosyncrasies that made their marriage special. When I caught up with Weil after the publication of her book *No Cheating, No Dying: I Had a Good Marriage. Then I Tried to Make it Better*, I asked if there was one lesson from the experiment that she most hoped to pass on to readers.

Her response was that it's worth it to make the effort. "And don't wait until you feel like you're in trouble to try to make it better," she said. "If you're in a good place, it's really easy to make it better from there. But if you wait until you're in a hole, it's really hard."

The sweet woman whose husband had filed for divorce found that to be true. Through tears, she told me that she would have done anything—*anything*—to stop the divorce from proceeding and to keep the family together for her children. It wasn't possible.

Yet even at that point, at the height of her agony, what she wanted her kids to know was that marriage can be wonderful. She hoped their belief in the institution wouldn't be shattered by their parents' divorce. And that they'd approach their own relationships with open hearts and the fortitude it takes to tackle difficult issues head on.

"It's the most wonderful thing in the world," she said of marriage. "It's such a treasure. I just wish I had known it's not as easy as it looks. I know that it's work—now I see that."

A Little Tenderness

I wasn't able to write about one of the most memorable couples I ever interviewed.

They both grew up in India. She was born into a wealthy, aristocratic family, had been educated at the finest private schools, and was expected to marry someone with the same pedigree. He lived on the lowest rung of India's caste system. A brilliant mathematical mind had earned him prestigious scholarships but didn't elevate him above the constraints of his ancestry.

Both were preparing for the same exam when a mutual friend arranged for the girl, whom I'll call Naya, to lend the boy, whom we'll refer to as Aziz, several expensive study guides. They were both seventeen. The two met for the exchange on a train platform in Mumbai—and then began to walk through the city. Soon they were going out almost weekly, always in secret, hiding among the crowds and sneaking onto rooftops, talking for hours. Before the end of a clandestine summer, they were in love.

She went off to university in England and he stayed in India. Neither knew where the relationship would lead—if either of their families found out, they would both be in serious trouble. But their connection was strong enough, across social classes and even oceans, that neither would let it slip away. After graduation they each made their way to Washington, D.C., where it became clear they would build a life together, despite the odds. Aziz had told his parents about Naya, and even brought her to meet them. They were charmed by the graceful young woman, but had deep concerns about the relationship and its repercussions. It could put Aziz in very real danger.

Naya had the same worries. Her older sister had married a financier, the son of family friends, and though it was a loveless marriage, it was one her parents approved of. As Naya approached her mid-twenties, the pressure for her to return to India and form a similar union was mounting. Her father and sister had both made trips to D.C. with the express purpose of convincing her to come home. Naya loved her family deeply but felt certain that if they found out about her relationship with Aziz, they'd plan to have him injured or killed if he ever returned to India.

I sat with Aziz and Naya in their efficiently decorated apartment the week after they had wed in secret. Aziz was deeply interested in aviation, so an officiant had led them through their vows at the Smithsonian National Air and Space Museum. Hordes of tourists acted as witnesses, since neither Aziz nor Naya planned to inform their families of the marriage. They just hoped it would provide legal protection for Aziz—and their union—in the United States.

It was hard to wrap my mind around everything these two young people, then just twenty-five, had gone through in order to be together. They were both brilliant, mature, and kind. And their love for each other was so sparklingly pure, it was difficult to imagine how anyone could object. But for them struggle was just a fact of life and love.

We spent three hours together and spoke several more times by phone. In the end I couldn't write their story for the *Post* because the couple understandably didn't want their names published. But I still felt lucky that I got to meet these two, and not just for the eye-opening window into the harsh realities some people face in the pursuit of love. Aziz and Naya embodied a kind of wisdom I'd rarely encountered before—one that can benefit all of us.

My jaw may have literally dropped when they talked about how they resolve arguments. "We hold hands whenever we have a disagreement," Aziz said. He explained that it keeps them in tune with each other, even when they're at odds, and prevents conflicts from escalating out of control. No one had ever taught them this habit—they'd come to it on their own—but there's a scientific basis for the benefits they described. A twenty-second hug, for example, has been proven to trigger the release of the bonding hormone oxytocin. There's a reason massages and backrubs bring the receiver such a rush of fondness for the giver. Touch makes us feel closer.

And in a study at the University of Virginia, researchers found that hand-holding significantly reduces stress. A group of married women were given mild electrical shocks while MRI machines captured the activity in their brains. When the women were told that a shock was about to be administered, their brains showed increased activity in areas that handle threats. But when the women held their spouses' hands—and, to a lesser degree, even a stranger's hand—they remained significantly calmer and less stressed. And later they described the experience as less unpleasant. So by holding hands when they disagreed, Naya and Aziz were unconsciously limiting the amount of stress hormones being released in their bodies. It's no wonder their arguments rarely spun out of control; they naturally felt less isolated and on guard. And I can only assume that with their hands occupied, they were less tempted to start throwing plates at each other.

Though Aziz and Naya faced incredible hardship in starting their life together, in many ways they seemed to be a step ahead of the rest of us. Theirs was a relationship built on love, dedication, and resolve.

No matter what trials come their way, I have faith that the two will be holding hands for decades to come.

Be Nice

Remember Betty and Edgar? The octogenarians who'd been married for more than sixty-five years after meeting on a blind date?

Toward the end of our interview I asked Betty, whose eyes twinkled above the thin tube pumping oxygen into her lungs, if she had advice for couples hoping for the kind of happy longevity she had shared with Edgar.

"Be nice!" she quickly shot back. "If you're going to be cruel, unkind, say mean things, it spoils immediately."

Be. Nice.

Back when their son was young, that meant that even if the two went to bed angry, they still kissed each other good night. When they were really frustrated, as I mentioned, he went into the garage to scream. She had a cigarette. Whatever the issue was, it eventually blew over. And when I met with them, "being nice" meant caring for each other through heart problems, liver damage, and emphysema. It meant pats on the knee, passing canes back and forth, and laughing at the same old jokes.

"Without a sense of humor, give up the ghost," Betty said. "If you can't laugh easily and cry easily, all is lost."

Be nice. It's what your first-grade teacher probably wrote at the top of the chalkboard. But the Golden Rule is easier to follow when you're sharing dolls or toy trucks with someone, rather than a whole life. Still, it's just as crucial.

Terri Orbuch, the sociology professor who's been tracking couples for decades to find out what makes them happy, found that small gestures make a huge difference. Brewing the morning coffee, touching the small of your partner's back, filling their car with gas. These things add up to more relationship satisfaction than a fancy dinner on Valentine's Day ever could. So does not calling each other names, belittling one another, or becoming disrespectful, even in moments of acrimony.

One long-married woman I interviewed emphasized the importance of being appreciative. When she came downstairs in the morning to find salt all over the oven, her initial reaction was annoyance that her husband hadn't wiped up the mess before leaving for work.

But over time she trained herself to look at the situation in a different way. She chose to be grateful that her husband made his own eggs in the morning, rather than expecting her to do it, and that he was careful to be quiet in the kitchen to avoid waking her. Even the little things, she said, deserve some thanks.

"You may not think that taking out the trash requires a thank-you," she told me. "Especially when it's their responsibility. Thank them anyway."

Be nice. It's an extraordinarily high standard. Probably an impossible one to maintain permanently. But it's a damn good goal.

Betty passed away a year after I met her. Her husband died the year after that. If kindness can offer the rest of us even a sliver of what they shared across six and a half decades of marriage, then it's worth a shot.

Keep It Confidential

After I'd been on the job several years, weddings and interviews occasionally ran together in my mind. But some couples, like Damon and Anika, are unforgettable. Yes, they were both thirty-five-year-old virgins when they married, but that is not the impressive part. Well, it's not the *only* impressive part. Toward the end of our interview, almost as an afterthought, they mentioned a pact they'd made not to discuss their marital issues with any friends or family members.

Think about that. Yes, it would be hard to abstain from sex for three and a half decades. But is it even *possible* to completely avoid venting about your spouse?

Damon and Anika explained that as part of their premarital counseling, they'd spent a weekend with a mentor couple in Ohio. There they talked about conflicts that had already arisen in the relationship and pledged that from that point on, whenever they found themselves at an impasse, they'd turn only to their mentor couple for complaints and feedback.

In their first year of marriage, for instance, when Anika wanted to get two dogs and Damon didn't want any, they called their mentors for help. After the couple helped Damon come to understand how fundamental canine companionship is to Anika's happiness, they brought home two puppies.

It wasn't that their mentor couple was necessarily smarter than anyone else they knew, or that they were particularly close to the pair. The idea, Anika explained, is to protect the union. If Anika were to turn to her mother or cousin with every complaint about Damon, they might begin to form a negative opinion of him. Because, of course, when we vent to friends and relatives, what we're usually looking for—and most often get—is reinforcement and support. "Oh, that's so awful. What is he *thinking*?" It's rare to find a confidant who's forthright and clear-minded enough to challenge you on your own behavior.

And while *you* may be able to forgive your partner after a tough argument, there's no guarantee the people you confided in will do the same. Which puts you in a pretty awkward position at the next family get-together.

Obviously most of us can't live by the same strict code as Damon and Anika. And venting about the little things can be cathartic, healthy, and humorous. But we can use their example to help us be more strategic in deciding what we share about our relationship, and with whom. If you have to get something off your chest, pick someone whose wisdom you really trust, and who isn't likely to spread the gossip to all your mutual acquaintances.

And then when things settle down, let your confidant know that you did not, in fact, marry a monster. If they're really a friend, they'll be glad to hear it.

Please, Thank You,
and Excuse Me

Bob and Henry met as servicemen during World War II, in the lounge of the Biltmore Hotel in Providence, Rhode Island. Two years later in Hawaii, Henry saw Bob's name on a poster for a play being put on by the USO. During intermission, he found Bob, who was as attractive as he'd remembered, and asked if he'd like to meet up. But then he got drunk, skipped the second half of the play, and missed their rendezvous.

"And I've never really forgotten that," Bob told me when I sat down with them in their penthouse apartment. "I was so good in the second act!"

It didn't matter. In 1948 Henry recognized Bob in a Baltimore watering hole. Bob had just moved to town and started a job in broadcasting. Henry had grown up in the city and lived nearby. When Bob mentioned that he was staying in a ramshackle boardinghouse, Henry invited him to sleep in his guest room for the night, promising, "Tomorrow we'll find you something."

That promise never came to fruition—from that day on the two were never apart. And sixty-two years later, after same-sex marriage was legalized in the District of Columbia, the pair finally wed on a rooftop overlooking the monuments. At the time, Henry was eighty-eight. Bob was eighty-nine. Their relationship had endured Henry's alcoholism and recovery, bigotry regarding their sexuality, and various health problems that plagued them both. Perhaps most challenging of all, it had survived the mundane struggles of coexistence.

"It's hard to live with yourself sometimes," Henry said. "Never mind for two strangers to live together and get used to each other."

But the decades of togetherness went by in a flash, they told me. Their immaculate apartment was decorated with art purchased on travels around the world. There were scrapbooks filled with memories. And in the living room two matching urns they'd already picked out for themselves were being put to use as bookends—and as a reminder that time was running short.

Bob and Henry were devoted theater patrons who never missed an opening night. They'd never officially "come out" but when they won an award for their support of the arts in 2008, Bob made the worst-kept secret in D.C. public knowledge.

"I have been greatly loved," he said in his acceptance

speech. "And I've loved greatly in return." Henry had been worried about how people would react—but then the crowd gave them a standing ovation.

"I think the reason it was so moving is that there were many in that audience who realized a relationship like ours could exist," Bob told me. "There was still hope that they could accumulate enough love between two people to make it last."

When I asked the pair their secret to staying together for all those years, the answer I got initially seemed so unromantic that I didn't even include it in my story. But it stayed with me.

The key, they said, was to be polite. To treat your partner with as much graciousness as you would a waitress or checkout clerk. When Bob sneezed, Henry always said, "God bless you." If Henry had to squeeze by Bob in the kitchen, he said, "Excuse me." They were steadfast in their manners, never forgetting "please," "thank you," or "you're welcome."

Their only other piece of advice was to enjoy the time together, even the disagreements. "You should have disagreements," Henry said. "It keeps it healthy." Enjoy all of it, he said, because it'll be gone "like that!"

He was right. Eight months after they exchanged vows in the summer sunshine, Bob died. But he passed knowing he'd been greatly loved—and that he'd loved greatly in return.

Love Means Having to Say
You're Sorry. A Lot.

I was obsessed with Erich Segal's *Love Story* as a teenager. I stole the book from my older sister when I was twelve and tortured my family by watching the movie on repeat throughout high school.

Beautiful, witty Jennifer Cavilleri became my idol. And while Oliver Barrett IV struck me as a little stiff and boring, I loved the way he loved her. I adored the sappy soundtrack and the scene where Jenny and Ollie fall for each other while making snow angels on the campus quad. If that was what college was like, I needed to skip a few grades to get there immediately.

And with every single viewing I bawled at the end. I don't think I ever read too much into the signature line—"Love means never having to say you're sorry"—but I was taken by the poetry of it.

I'm not saying I'm proud of any of this. I'm saying if you're a fifteen-year-old girl who can't so much as land a first kiss, you'd watch a lot of tearjerkers, too.

Years later, sitting at other people's weddings, I heard a lot about the word *sorry*. Ministers and rabbis and priests love to take a few minutes to offer marriage advice. They usually start by talking about love and God and the winding paths that brought these two people together. Then they talk about how to *stay* together. Weekend after weekend, I listened as officiants instructed couples to learn to say they're sorry and to forgive— and to do it over and over again. Apparently they did not share my obsession with *Love Story*.

But of course they're right. As that great sage of our time, Kathy Lee Gifford, put it, "Love in the real world means saying you're sorry ten times a day." Maybe she could get away with just eight apologies if she put down the goblet of Chablis in the morning, but you get the point.

A Zogby International Poll of 7,590 people found that the willingness to atone is a key component to lasting love. The survey discovered that married people were twice as likely as their single, separated, or divorced counterparts to cough up an apology, even when they didn't think they were actually to blame.

That doesn't mean tossing out a terse "Sor-*ry*." After reading Randy Pausch's bestseller, *The Last Lecture*, my husband, Aaron, became a stickler about the way to express a meaningful apology. You should see the look on his face if I even try to start a sentence with "I'm sorry if you feel . . ."

And apparently he's not alone. A Stanford University study interviewed sixty couples about their relationship satisfaction and then tracked them for a week, asking participants to keep track of negative events, whether they prompted an apology and if the issue was resolved. The researchers found that happiness in a relationship wasn't directly correlated to the number of apologies, but to the sincerity of the mea culpa. The people who were most content were more likely to receive apologies in which their partner actually expressed responsibility for their misdeed. As Benjamin Franklin said, "Never ruin an apology with an excuse."

But the burden of reparation doesn't just rest with the guilty party. The aggrieved has to soften, too. In *The Seven Principles for Making Marriage Work,* John Gottman writes about the importance of what he calls "repair attempts." These often come up in the midst of an argument when one person tries to make a joke or concession in an attempt to defuse the situation.

"The success or failure of a couple's repair attempts is one of the primary factors in whether a marriage flourishes or flounders," according to Gottman. If we want to be excused for our imperfections and personal failings, then we'd better be ready to offer the same grace to our partners.

Concessions and absolutions don't need to come immediately. And, despite the old adage, they don't even need to come before you go to sleep. Sometimes it's probably best for everyone if you and your fury just shuffle off to bed. The important thing is that the resolution does come eventually. And that it comes with a willingness to move on without holding grudges or counting wrongs. Because whoever is keeping score will likely lose in the end.

I still think it's nice that Jenny and Ollie never needed to say "I'm sorry." Unfortunately, you and I and Kathy Lee Gifford definitely do.

For the Kids

Legendary basketball coach John Wooden once wrote the following: "The best thing a father can do for his children is to love their mother."

I think this is true. And that it goes both ways.

Don't Worry About the Joneses

Chrisanna Northrup was a San Diego mother of three who expected more from her fifteen-year marriage. "I pictured more passion, more fun, more love," she told me.

When the disappointment grew, she moved out. Two years of couples counseling did little to quell the fighting between her and her husband.

In her moments of exasperation, she wondered what, exactly, was normal in relationships. What was a typical amount of fighting? Of sex? Of happiness? Instead of continuing to wonder, Chrisanna, a blond dynamo with a megawatt smile, decided to find out. She recruited the help of two renowned social scientists and created a 1,300-question online survey that was taken by more than seventy thousand readers of the *Huffington Post, Reader's Digest,* and other media outlets.

The study yielded interesting results, which Chrisanna and

her coauthors culled into the book *The Normal Bar.* They found that 74 percent of people are happy with their relationships and that only 15 percent admit to having an affair. (Although interestingly, when an "affair" was defined as "sex outside your current relationship," the number rose to 33 percent of men and 19 percent of women.)

The couples with the highest rates of satisfaction tended to exhibit certain behaviors, including hand-holding, kissing, saying "I love you," going on date nights, and using pet names. So Chrisanna started calling her husband "sweetheart" and adopted several other new habits that she credits with helping to save her marriage.

While I was very happy to hear that Chrisanna's journey had had such a lovely outcome, I wondered whether her initial query—"What's normal?"—was actually a helpful one.

We know instinctively that it's dangerous to compare one sibling to another or your own kids to somebody else's off-spring. And once we leave high school, we're usually able to lose at least *some* of the myopia that forces us to constantly measure ourselves against whoever is in our vicinity. Is he richer than me? Is she prettier? But the tendency to compare our relationships to others is equally insidious and damaging.

It's human nature to look at how other people operate in-side romantic partnerships. It's what I do, after all, and the point of this book to some degree. Relationships are mysteri-ous and private, so we want to get behind the curtain. And certainly it can be instructive to learn from those couples we admire, trying to incorporate some of their best practices into our own lives.

But the danger comes when we start judging another couple's relationship as superior or inferior to our own. Or when we assume we have the first clue about what goes on between those two people. Because we don't.

Does anybody actually know what your relationship is about? What it's *really about*, when no when else is looking? Of course not. No one else understands your inside jokes or lingering grudges. No one else knows how he comforted you in your deepest agony. Or how she kicked you when you were down in a way you'll never quite forget. Whatever exists between two people can never fully be known outside their tiny circle. That's the beauty of marriage.

Yes, he pops up to clear the dishes whenever company is over for dinner. But maybe he turns away from her in bed, when she longs to be held. She packs him lunch with a note that says "I love you" every single day, but she might also invite the UPS man in for more than just coffee. Isn't it always the couples who appear to have it all together who end up falling apart?

And envying another relationship can undermine the way we value our own. Rather than spending mental energy focused on what's so great about those other two, we'd be better off thinking about the many ways in which our own partner is wonderful. Studies have shown that people who idealize their mates—concentrating on their good qualities rather than the bad—are happier in their marriages than those without rose-colored glasses.

Of course, you're not going to see your spouse as flawless. You live with this person, after all. But you can make a choice to cultivate gratitude for this totally imperfect, perfectly unique relationship that belongs only to the two of you. And let the neighbors worry about themselves.

Let's Talk About Sex

I interviewed Oprah's favorite sex therapist, Laura Berman, right before her new television series was about to debut. One of the first episodes they taped was about a woman who could only reach orgasm by rubbing herself against the rounded corner of an upside-down laundry basket. How could a show get any better? (In fact, it may have peaked too early. Get it? Sorry.)

I found Berman to be instantly likable—smart and warm. She told me how frequently she's approached at cocktail parties and on airplanes by people who want to know the answer to some version of this question: "Am I normal?" (Yes, you are. Relax.) The second most common inquiry was something like: "How often should I be having sex with my spouse?"

Berman's answer: "Whenever you or your partner initiates it."

There's no magic number or formula. Her suggestion was that, if possible, people should simply *try* to be generous with each other in this regard.

Obviously there are a thousand and one factors that can complicate the intimacy between any two people, even when they love each other deeply. Infertility, mismatched libidos, erectile dysfunction, hormone imbalances, harried lives, and the exhaustion that comes from caring for children or aging parents are just the start.

But as a general rule of thumb, I thought Berman's advice made sense. The Internet is full of confessionals from couples who undertake challenges to have sex every day for a week or a month or a year. This is an extreme. But the takeaway from just about every account is that having sex—even when one person, or both, isn't quite in the mood—has a positive effect on the relationship. It brings the two people in question closer and makes them more interested in intimacy the next time around. (I'm pretty sure this is what Isaac Newton meant when he wrote about bodies in motion tending to stay in motion.)

Just say yes—if you can. It's a theory worth putting to practice the next time your partner tries to lure you into the bedroom.

What Makes It Last

There may not be a single secret to ensure a long, happy marriage, but scientists have identified some behaviors that help sustain a relationship over the years. Here are some of the best tips their studies offer:

1. Go tandem hang-gliding. Okay, you don't actually have to take to the skies, but anything you can do to generate excitement together helps. Of course there should be regular date nights, but researchers have found that what's even more effective is trying new things together—taking a class, traveling someplace interesting, eating at a previously unexplored ethnic restaurant. Activities that create interesting experiences mimic the excitement that comes naturally, early in relationships. So you can recapture the blush of young romance with your same-old spouse just by breaking out of routine. (And just FYI,

there is also some evidence that women feel a little friskier outside the homestead.)

2. Be kind five times a day. Only be a jerk once. Gottman and other researchers have found that happy couples have a 5:1 ratio of positive to negative interactions. Unfortunately, the human brain registers bad stuff that happens to us much more acutely than the good. The good news, according to Gottman, is that people can actually store up reserves of positive feelings to carry them through the hard times.

3. Maintain eye contact. Or hand contact. Or any other kind of contact. Anything you can do to feel connected—and it doesn't have to be sex—increases levels of oxytocin, the bonding hormone, which, as I've said previously, helps boost that loving feeling.

4. Drink more champagne. Or do an actual victory dance. Celebrate your partner's successes at every turn. A study out of the University of California, Santa Barbara, showed that intimacy and marital satisfaction increase when spouses share and rejoice in each other's achievements. Of course, it's crucial to support one another through the bad times, but it's just as important (and usually more fun) to toast life's sweeter moments.

5. Keep it light. Laughing at any time releases feel-good hormones and correlates to happier marriages. But it's a

particularly useful tool when deployed in the midst of an argument. If you can cut the tension with a funny face or self-deprecating joke, you can stop the fight from escalating.

6. Go to church or temple or into nature together. There is some evidence that couples who pray together really are more likely to stay together. But as rates of interfaith marriage skyrocket, there's at least a fair chance your and your beloved's religious origins won't be aligned. Don't worry. The important part is to find shared meaning in life and to create rituals that support those beliefs, whether that's in a soaring cathedral or on a peaceful beach.

7. Write in your gratitude journal. Being thankful for all that's good about your partner generates more positivity between the two of you. Does your husband take the bus to work each day so that there'll be more money to put in the kids' college savings fund? Does your wife make the house smell nice in ways you don't quite understand? Focus on that, instead of the mess on their side of the bedroom.

8. Do the dishes. Both of you. According to a 2007 survey by the Pew Research Center, sharing domestic duties was among the top three factors associated with a successful marriage. It ranked higher than having mutual interests, good housing, or an adequate income. The only issues that

ranked higher were faithfulness and a satisfying sex life. So make whoopee—with each other—and then offer to fold the laundry.

9. Keep up. Your spouse will change. Perhaps not in the ways that you expect, but they'll change nonetheless. As author Mignon McLaughlin put it, "A successful marriage requires falling in love many times, always with the same person." Or at least an updated version of the same person, which means talking to them with as much curiosity as you did when you first started dating. Gottman gets at this with the idea of "love mapping," or understanding your spouse's world. What are their biggest stresses? Their major aspirations? Orbuch points to the same idea with her daily ten-minute conversations. You might be surprised to find out exactly who's sitting across from you at the breakfast table today. Hopefully the investigation will give you the chance to fall in love all over again.

10. Say "I love you." Obviously

A Test of Endurance

When Leila tied the knot on New Year's Eve, 1979, she didn't think the marriage would last. She was a world traveler and bohemian who came from a long line of divorcées. Broken marriages were, she said, something of a family tradition.

"My thought was, 'If it doesn't work out, I can get divorced,'" she told me.

But she and Tony, an aspiring actor, made it through the early years, when he was auditioning in New York and she was working as a television reporter in Pennsylvania. Doctors told Leila she couldn't have children, but after four years, she gave birth to a "miracle baby." Their daughter struggled right from the start, and was soon diagnosed with a host of conditions, including mental retardation, autism, and a seizure disorder.

Suddenly life could no longer be lived on a whim. Their little girl required constant care and even into her teens and twenties would sleep just a few hours at a time, and only when Tony lay down on the floor near her bed. With no family and little nearby support, the couple never vacationed, rarely went out to dinner, and had virtually no time to themselves. They both gave up professions they loved for careers that would offer more stability.

They loved their daughter immensely, but the experience was more grueling than anyone but the two of them would ever understand. It taxed their marriage tremendously and left both of them privately wondering, at times, if they'd be better off on their own. But, as Tony said, "We had the resolve to resolve everything that happened in our relationship." They even adopted a little boy who'd been in foster care and, when their daughter was ten, got another surprise: Leila was pregnant again, this time with a healthy baby boy.

The pair stuck it out in part, they said, because they were in the trenches together. No one else could even begin to contemplate what they'd endured. And though at times they chafed against each other and the constraints of their life, they'd battled through it together.

By the time I met with them, a few months shy of their thirty-first anniversary, their daughter was living nearby with a full-time caregiver. One son was in college; the other would be on his way the next year. The pair was starting to breathe again. They could go to movies and sleep in on Saturday mornings. Tony was even starting to audition for local acting gigs. And what surprised them most was not just that they'd made it to the three-decade mark, but how much they enjoyed their relationship now.

"What I like to share with people in new relationships is that old relationships are really nice. You become very, very close friends," Leila told me. "I say, 'Hang in there, because if you work through it, what you get on the other side is something that you can't even imagine—it's a very beautiful thing.'"

I heard something similar from a colleague whose parents always seemed to be at each other's throats while she was growing up. Then, a decade or so after everyone was out of the house, and life revolved around afternoon matinees and visits with grandchildren, it suddenly seemed like they were attached at the hip.

There are rewards for simply enduring. A fascinating study by the National Fatherhood Initiative found that 13 percent of adults had seriously contemplated divorce during their previous three years of marriage. But of those people who had once considered their marriage to be seriously on the rocks, 94 percent reported being happy they stuck it out.

In another study, this one sponsored by the (decidedly pro-marriage) Institute for American Values, 10 percent of the people they surveyed described themselves as being unhappy in their marriages and another 2 percent said they were "very unhappy." Those couples were followed over the next five years and 15 percent of them divorced. The other 85 percent stayed together. What's really interesting is that of those unhappy adults who stayed together, two-thirds of them reported being happy in their marriage five years later. And 75 percent of those who were "very unhappy," but didn't divorce after five years, now described themselves as happily married.

Some people marry the wrong person. And we can probably all point to others who are nourished and satisfied by a second marriage in ways they never could have been in their first. But for those who have a marriage founded on love and friendship that now seems lost, it might be worth waiting to see if the warmth returns. I once read that the key to a long marriage is "not wanting a divorce at the same time." They should print that on wedding cards. I would buy a dozen.

Because divorce, as anyone who's been through it will tell you, is among the most traumatic experiences one can endure in life. Besides scar tissue, there's no guarantee of what you'll find on the other side. And if children are involved, the pain of the fission is multiplied beyond calculation.

That doesn't mean it's not the right decision. It may very well be, especially in instances of abuse or chronic neglect.

It just means that for some couples, there is a light at the end of the tunnel. And while the grass may look greener on the other side of the fence, they should remember that they're in a tunnel and there shouldn't be fences in tunnels. So it's probably just an illusion.

Everybody loves to see an elderly couple walking hand in hand in the park. And we all hope to be that lucky someday. But perhaps, in the end, it had more to do with endurance than luck.

Better to Have Loved and Lost

Facebook posts of food don't often drive me to tears. But this one did; it depicted a couple of Filipino eggrolls with sweet-and-sour sauce, and the caption read: "Thank you Erwin Lobo for making these and freezing them." Erwin had died two years earlier. But he was still finding a way to take care of his husband, Ed, and their two young sons.

I knew when I started on the weddings beat that not all of the marriages I wrote about would last. But I was prepared for them to end with divorce, not death. And especially not for young couples in their prime, like Ed and Erwin. But it's these pairs—whose dreams are cut unfathomably short—who have the most important lessons to teach. Like life itself, love is never guaranteed to last another day, but it's always worth the risk.

By the time I met him, Erwin was thirty-seven years old and knew he didn't have much time left. He was listless and weak as he recalled his first date with Ed, ten years earlier. Erwin had just moved to New York City from the Philippines and came across Ed's profile on a dating site. Logical, detail-oriented Ed listed his specifications for an ideal partner—a man who was under six feet tall, Christian, and interested in starting a family.

After getting lost on the subway, Erwin showed up an hour late to the coffee shop where they'd agreed to meet. But when they sat down to dinner after, and Ed reached across the table to hold hands, "I suddenly felt connected to him," Erwin told me. "Right from the start, I felt like we'd been doing this a long, long time."

Within a year they were talking about marriage and after two years together they started planning for a family. After a prolonged adoption process they brought home one little boy from Guatemala. Three years later another boy made them a family of four. They moved to the suburbs, went all out on Christmas decorations, and ate together almost every night. It was the family life Ed had always dreamed of having.

Then Erwin developed back pain that turned out to be lung cancer. With round after round of chemotherapy and radiation, it seemed for a while that Erwin might be able to beat the odds. But the cancer kept coming back.

"When you're dating somebody, you just don't think about this type of thing," Ed said of the illness. "You think of that as being a million years away." It was wrenching and exhausting and made every moment exceedingly precious.

A year and a half after receiving the diagnosis, the pair exchanged vows in a beautiful, sunlit garden before fifty guests and their two sons. Erwin cried as he made his way down the aisle. He called the event "a celebration of life."

"I'm very, very lucky," he told me. "A lot of people just leave their homes and get shot or get in an accident. They won't have the chance to say goodbye to their families." What weighed on him most, he said, was the thought of no longer being able to care for his family. "That's why I'll hold on until I can't."

Eleven months later he let go. But not before he put a batch of spring rolls in the freezer. "Erwin is probably the most giving person that I have ever met in my life," Ed said before they got married. "No one has to ask anything of him. He's just there with what's needed." Even when he was gone, he'd found a way to be there.

Lori expected her husband, Dan, to be with her for a lifetime after they got married. Like Ed and Erwin, they met online. Lori was in her mid-thirties, then, and had spent the previous decade immersed in her technology career. At the behest of friends, she finally created an eHarmony profile, if only to prove to them that online dating wouldn't work for her. But one of the first messages she received was from Dan, a brilliant NASA scientist who wanted her to know up front that a flag-football injury during high school had left him paralyzed from the chest down.

Dating a guy in a wheelchair "hadn't been in my realm of possibilities," Lori recalled. But she "wasn't going to let it be a deal breaker. . . . I was willing to figure out if we were actually compatible and work through the whole dating thing and let it fall out that way."

Over dinner she found him to be almost intimidatingly smart, and subsequent phone conversations revealed a teasing, warm chemistry that left the pretty redhead laughing nonstop. She tried to learn everything she could about the way his world worked and soon the chair and the physical limitations faded into the background. Five months after they met, the two were engaged. She sat on his lap as he wheeled into their wedding reception.

Lori knew nothing about the honeymoon Dan had planned—five weeks in Europe, traveling France, Greece, Turkey, Rome, and London.

"It was definitely a trip of a lifetime," Lori told me later. "We just never thought it would be *the* trip of a lifetime." Two years later a pain in Dan's side was revealed to be pneumonia.

"Come on, you guys are smart," Lori remembers Dan saying to his doctors as he lay in the hospital. "You can do this—be positive. Don't give up on me. I'm not giving up." But his organs failed and there was nothing his physicians could do. He died the day before Lori's thirty-ninth birthday.

I caught up with Lori a little over a year after Dan's passing. She was still racked with grief, but even through the haze of sorrow, her perspective on their love was inspiring. She told me that she counted her blessings every day for having had the chance to know Dan. "He was my biggest fan and would have done anything for me. He set the bar high."

Their relationship, even in spite of its premature ending, "was a gift," she said. "A very good gift."

As we talked, I couldn't help but think about a Garth Brooks song about taking the gamble to love: "Life is not tried, it is merely survived / If you're standing outside the fire." None of us knows what the next breath will bring. Our relationships could sour or crumble. The time we have with our loved ones could be cut tragically short. And the only small measure of recourse at our disposal is to appreciate whatever goodness we have, for as long as we have it.

In the end, Lori said, Dan "taught me what's really important in life, and how precious time really is.

"So how you spend it, and who you spend it with, is what matters."

Afterword

I wrote this book while I was pregnant and revised it while caring for an infant. I mention this by way of explaining that all errors, inaccuracies, and sloppy turns of phrase are exclusively Sadie's fault.

I also mention it because, in addition to being my coauthor, Sadie was my intended audience. As I type these words, she's beside me, asleep in her crib, chubby six-month-old hands curled up in the soft evening light. My hope is that the lessons in this book will be of use to her, and to anyone else who reads it. That some tiny insight will prove helpful and true and will make life and love that much sweeter.

Not long ago my family gathered to celebrate my parents' fortieth anniversary. It was the kind of lavish affair that included hot dogs, a case of Miller Lite, and a charcoal grill that four grown men struggled to operate.

Forty years. We're not a sentimental clan, but the occasion

still felt momentous. They'd made it. They'd built something that was solid enough to survive all the challenges that come with life in general, and romantic relationships in particular.

I always felt lucky to have grown up under the protective cover of my parents' marriage. It's never worn any mask of perfection, but it is founded on mutual respect, laughter, and abiding friendship. And to me it felt like safety, in the highest sense of the word.

Aaron's parents have an equally strong marriage, so I feel doubly thankful. He and I both came to our own union having witnessed true commitment up close. We saw what it was like to occasionally want to throttle someone even as you count your lucky stars they're around. We saw what it was like to know who you're coming home to and who you can rely on.

My deep prayer is that Aaron and I will be able to give Sadie that same gift—and it is a gift, probably one of the most valuable a person can receive. (And one, to be sure, that can be provided by all parents, including the especially strong ones raising children on their own.) It's precious beyond measure to know that the glue holding your family together is durable, that you can weather tough times together and that love can endure even as it ebbs and flows, flexes and morphs.

We'll rely on the examples of our parents and on the knowledge of those who've gone before us, including the couples mentioned in this book. I am profoundly grateful to all the people who shared their stories with me and became my great teachers. I hope that I have honored their generosity by passing their wisdom along.

Love will always hold wonder and mystery. But what we know for sure is that it's our lifeblood. Whether it's the love of our family, friends, pets, or spouses, our days and years have little meaning without it. So our work is to create it, protect it, and to share it with reckless abandon. And to do so with the certainty that it will be returned to us in ways we can't yet imagine.

So, my closing wish is this: May your life be filled with great love—beautiful, abundant, and everlasting.

Acknowledgments

I'd like to thank all of my friends, family, and colleagues for their support and encouragement throughout the years. I am profoundly lucky to have you all in my life.

The following list is by no means exhaustive, but I wanted to highlight a few of the people who were particularly instrumental to the publication of *The Real Thing.* Thank you to my indomitable agent, Esther Newberg, who championed this book from the start and who, frankly, I feel fortunate to have had the opportunity to meet, much less work with. And to ICM's Zoe Sandler, who is just wonderful.

I am deeply grateful to my three extraordinarily talented editors, Hannah Elnan, Joey McGarvey, and Nina Shield. (I churned through three editors not, I hope, because I was such a difficult edit, but because they kept getting engaged and moving away. Magic book, perhaps?) Thank you to the whole Ballantine team, who made my inaugural journey into the publishing world a joy. And I greatly appreciate the work of three women who made this book beautiful: Victoria Allen and Dana Blanchette of Random House, and Michele Hatty Fritz of Meant To Be Calligraphy.

Thank you, also, to my early readers and great friends, whose feedback and guidance on the manuscript was invaluable: Sara Gebhardt, Nicholas Johnston, Rachel Dry, and Amy Joyce. And to the following for their help in countless other ways: Pat and Judi McCarthy; Ann, Ryan, Jack, and Leah Werzyn; Carla, Paul, Rachel, and Leah Rosenthal; Marin and Ellie Strisik; Michael McCarthy and Cara Brandon; Neil Irwin; Erin Johnston; Bridget Scannell; Kathleen Jedrosko; Bill McQuillen; Amy Argetsinger; Sarah Halzack; Steve and Tara Goldenberg; Marvin Joseph; Suzanna Sanchez; and Beth Broadwater.

I am forever grateful to my husband, Aaron—he believed in me and in this book and he made me believe, too. He was my constant sounding board, my ultimate champion, and my greatest source of comfort throughout this process. I also appreciate his willingness to go to Mommy & Me swim classes when I needed to stay home and write. And thank you to our sweet Sadie for her great company, good cheer, and flawless editorial judgment.

Finally, I am enormously indebted to all the couples who let me into their lives. I continue to be honored that you trusted me with your stories—and hope, most of all, that I did you justice.

Bibliography

Brunell, Amy B., Michael H. Kernis, Brian M. Goldman, Whitney Heppner, Patricia Davis, Edward V. Cascio, and Gregory D. Webster. "Dispositional Authenticity and Romantic Relationship Functioning." *Personality and Individual Differences.*

Cable, N., M. Bartley, T. Chandola, and A. Sacker. "Friends Are Equally Important to Men and Women, but Family Matters More for Men's Well-being." *Journal of Epidemiology & Community Health,* December 6, 2013.

Coan, James A., Hillary S. Schaefer, and Richard J. Davidson. "Lending a Hand: Social Regulation of the Neural Response to Threat." *Psychological Science.*

Dyrenforth, Portia S., Deborah A. Kashy, M. Brent Donnellan, and Richard E. Lucas. "Predicting Relationship and Life Satisfaction from Personality in Nationally Representative Samples from Three Countries: The Relative Importance of Actor, Partner, and Similarity Effects." *Journal of Personality and Social Psychology.*

Finkel, E. J., E. B. Slotter, L. B. Luchies, G. M. Walton, and J. J. Gross. "A Brief Intervention to Promote Conflict Reappraisal Preserves Marital Quality Over Time." *Psychological Science,* December 9, 2013.

Finkel, E. J., P. W. Eastwick, B. R. Karney, H. T. Reis, and S. Sprecher, "Online Dating: A Critical Analysis from the Perspective of Psychological Science." *Psychological Science in the Public Interest.*

Fisher, H. E., L. L. Brown, A. Aron, G. Strong, and D. Mashek. "Reward, Addiction, and Emotion Regulation Systems Associated with Rejection in Love." *Journal of Neurophysiology,* Vol. 104, No. 1., 2010.

Gable, Shelly L., Harry T. Reis, Emily A. Impett, and Evan R. Asher. "What Do You Do When Things Go Right?: The Intrapersonal and Interpersonal Benefits of Sharing Positive Events." *Journal of Personality and Social Psychology.*

Hira, S. N., and N. C. Overall. "Improving Intimate Relationships: Targeting the Partner Versus Changing the Self." *Journal of Social and Personal Relationships,* December 14, 2011.

Johnson, Matthew D., and Jared R. Anderson. "The Longitudinal Association of Marital Confidence, Time Spent Together, and Marital Satisfaction." *Family Process.*

Lavner, Justin A., Benjamin R. Karney, and Thomas N. Bradbury. "Newlyweds' Optimistic Forecasts of Their Marriage: For Better or for Worse?" *Journal of Family Psychology.*

Lewandowski, Gary. "Promoting Positive Emotions Following Relationship Dissolution Through Writing." *The Journal of Positive Psychology.*

Schumann, K. "Does Love Mean Never Having to Say You're Sorry?: Associations Between Relationship Satisfaction, Perceived Apology Sincerity, and Forgiveness." *Journal of Social and Personal Relationships,* December 28, 2012.

Slotter, E. B., W. L. Gardner, and E. J. Finkel. "Who Am I Without You?: The Influence of Romantic Breakup on the Self-Concept." *Personality and Social Psychology Bulletin,* Vol. 36, No. 2., 2010.

Wedekind, Claus, Thomas Seebeck, Florence Bettens, and Alexander J. Paepke. "MHC-Dependent Mate Preferences in Humans." *Proceedings of the Royal Society B: Biological Sciences.*

About the Author

ELLEN MCCARTHY is a feature writer for *The Washington Post*. She started her career at the *Post* in 2000 and covered business, technology, arts, and entertainment before launching the paper's On Love section. She's interviewed hundreds of couples and for four years spent almost all of her Saturday nights lurking in the shadows of other people's weddings. She lives in Washington, D.C., with her husband and daughter.

@EllenMcCarthy

About the Type

This book was set in Baskerville, a typeface designed by John Baskerville (1706–75), an amateur printer and typefounder, and cut for him by John Handy in 1750. The type became popular again when the Lanston Monotype Corporation of London revived the classic roman face in 1923. The Mergenthaler Linotype Company in England and the United States cut a version of Baskerville in 1931, making it one of the most widely used typefaces today.